ENGLISH CATHEDRALS

ENGLISH CATHEDRALS

WITH A
FOREWORD BY
GEOFFREY GRIGSON

PHOTOGRAPHS
AND INTRODUCTION BY MARTIN HÜRLIMANN
DESCRIPTIVE TEXT BY PETER MEYER

THAMES AND HUDSON · LONDON

PUBLISHED MAY 1950
REPRINTED AUG. 1950
REPRINTED MAR. 1951
REPRINTED JULY 1953

ALL RIGHTS RESERVED

PRODUCED BY THAMES AND HUDSON LIMITED LONDON
PRINTED AND BOUND IN GREAT BRITAIN BY JARROLD AND SONS LIMITED
GRAVURE PLATES PRINTED IN SWITZERLAND BY GEBR. FRETZ A.G. ZURICH

FOREWORD

WHEN I was a child living in a remote vicarage in the country the only building on a large scale of which I had any experience was the theatre in the nearest town to which we went for the pantomime. The experience, if it was not religious, was at least mysterious, the experience of the great dark auditorium in which there was no illumination except that green light following the evil face of the witch down below. It was a Regency theatre with a portico enclosed by great pillars. I remember my feelings of awe at the white immensity of these pillars, feelings I never regained until I stepped down into the nave at Durham. There are limits to the imaginative effect of secular buildings. Secular poetry, secular music or painting, yes, they may now and again embody the greater depth of experience. But buildings have a purpose, and immense buildings have a public purpose, usually, and most public purposes are limited in their imaginative action. There is less difference between an immense factory and the most splendid castle than there is between the most splendid castle and a cathedral. A splendid building designed to house a prince or designed for a parliament is—a splendid building; and not, I rather think, much more. Purity, intricacy, subtlety of proportions? No doubt. But sublime order is a bit too much like a sublime skeleton, and I am fairly sure that the cathedrals which protrude so immensely out of the Middle Ages, alone raise architecture up to the higher peaks of imagination.

Mr. Hürlimann, who has taken the fine photographs in this book, makes a good point when he says that Englishmen find their cathedrals strange and foreign. But it is not only the strangeness of something born of another kind of Christianity. It is the strangeness and monumentality of the greatest art. Not many streets from Durham or Wells or Ely cathedral there will be a cinema and a cheap store, which are among the representative buildings of our time. How, without feeling that we encounter something most alien, do we make the transition now from these into the nave or choir? The cathedrals have been abstracted from the faith and the sense of divine glory by which they were raised. They have also lost their furnishings, they have lost their shrines, their statues, the colours which spread over the stone. They are reduced in a cold way perhaps to the stony elements of their architectural grandeur, though whether "reduced" is the apt word I am not quite certain. The spirit, the fire, which established the lantern at Ely, or poised screen beyond screen at Gloucester, or contrived those shadowed recesses on the west front above the houses and stores and cinemas of Peterborough, or deposited those Old Testament Pillars deep into the floor at Durham or sent the marble lines of the Chapel of the Nine Altars of Durham streaking upward beyond the choir, is nearly as remote from us now as the spirit which added up the stones at Karnak or Paestum or in the Yucatanese jungles. There is so much to increase the difficulty of appreciation; and I rather think there can be no other works of art of the same order of magnificence which influence most of us in our lives so little. Mr. T. S. Eliot has remarked of Shakespeare that when a poet is so great, we must have aid in judging of his greatness: "We need both the opinions of other poets and the divers views of critics in order to help us to understand." We need every help we can get to understand the cathedrals, and so far as my reading goes we have far less help than such a magnificence of spiritual embodiment deserves and requires. Analysis of style and architectural description may help, and plenty has been published, but imaginative performance needs imaginative criticism. Should I be far wrong if I said we simply have no book on English cathedrals which does what ought to be done, imaginatively? The cathedrals are far less fortunate than Milton or Shakespeare. With little help of the deeper kind we have to discover each for ourselves the audacities of cathedral after cathedral. Yet skilful photographs such as Mr. Hürlimann's can help us and give us delight, both in prospect and retrospect.

He has looked at the seventeen cathedrals of his choice with an eye accustomed to the medieval architecture of other countries. I think that points for us his vision, his praise, and his reservations. The reservations are few. The vertical grandeur of Beauvais, the elegance raised into sublimity, is of one kind, the intricate creation of space beyond space in the English cathedrals is of another. In the French cathedrals I feel more a sense of the accepted universality of the divine; the glory is here, everywhere, and these slender immensities, these remote vaults, embody it. In the English cathedrals, and especially in Gloucester, I have the feeling that beyond one more veil of stone, the secret of everything will be revealed. But I have not any desire (and I suspect far too many of my countrymen have) to race the French and English buildings in a cultural point-to-point, in which it is foregone that the English will lose. The different cathedrals are the imaginative and religious expression, within one religion, of two different peoples. And the point of comparing them is to discover the special vitalities and excellences of each. That is too obvious, no doubt, but at least for ourselves it does need to be said over and over again, and the sensitive reactions of a foreigner will help us to settle our own unnecessary doubts.

When I received the Swiss edition of Mr. Hürlimann's book, I was curious about two things: would he illustrate one piece, from Gloucester, of the most fearless and faultless virtuosity in stone that I had encountered, and what would his photographs make of Durham? Plate 104 gives the answer about Gloucester; and how, I may ask, do we contrive to enter into the full experience of men who conceived that fantastic support to a vaulted roof, that marvellous tension between the rising and descending stems which imparts to the heaviness of stone a grace, a function, and a refined strength altogether beyond the natural order of things? I had lately been to Durham, and was struck by the tameness of such photographs of the nave as I had seen contrasted with the immediate effect, the huge effect, the moment one goes in through the door, of those ordered and gigantic trunks of sandstone. And I found (Plate 164) that Mr. Hürlimann had caught that effect to a degree beyond other photographers.

It does not abash me at all that the sculpture of the English cathedrals is short of what we experience in France or Germany. As I look through these photographs, as I go through the cathedrals, how possessive and splendid are the contrasts and surprises of structure, the dramatic activities of space and of shape, Hereford (Plate 113), Gloucester (Plate 107), Wells (Plate 94), Salisbury (Plates 73 and 74), Ely (Plate 40). It is curious to see again and again some abstract motive which independently and too abstractedly reappears in the work of the better sculptors of our day, and then to calculate that force which enabled the cathedral builders to invent not one, but hundreds of such motives and to combine them, out of the extravagance and variety of their power, in these gigantic and netted organisms of imagination. They did not care for mountains or caves in the Middle Ages, and why should they have done when they had the will and the power to create cave-and-mountain in one, exquisitely ordered, and inhabited neither by troll nor demon? A country sparsely occupied by people who were infants in technology compared with ourselves were able to imagine and create these cathedrals. Built so many years ago, it may be humiliating to reflect that in mere size, they are still by and large the most massive and monumental achievements of English architecture. In the way the world is and promises to be, we cannot conceive that men will ever be able to erect buildings again to rival them. These reflections may be humiliating, but it is something to belong to the human species when, possessed by a great idea, it has been capable of so much.

GEOFFREY GRIGSON

INTRODUCTION

MANY Englishmen find their cathedrals a bit strange, something belonging more to continental Europe than the British Isles. They point to the parish church, which more clearly than the pompous monumentality of the cathedrals represents the kind of architecture expressive of the country and the people. Indeed by its function the parish church is more essentially, more intimately linked with the Englishman's life: for a thousand years his Sunday observance has centred in the church, the architecture of which in its provincial independence could develop exactly in accord with the slow, steady growth of an insular tradition. The cathedrals are different. They are landmarks which all over Europe, from Uppsala in the north to Famagusta in the south, proclaim the triumph of the *Una Sancta Ecclesia Catholica* of the Christian Middle Ages. Their great walls and towers overtop the old cities, and they embody even now in Germany, France, Spain, Italy, England, that unity of the west which in the Crusades was for once the brotherhood-in-arms of the kings, the knights, and the soldiers of Europe. The influence of the great cathedral workshops, and the architects themselves, passed from country to country, and although every one of these gigantic enterprises was a monument of the joyous faith and willing sacrifice of one particular city and nation, the strong individuality of the builders themselves was devoted always to the one great object of the west. As the communion of faith and form took different shape in the different countries, so its leitmotiv varied more richly always, more daringly and originally. The English cathedrals are a most impressive example of this. As the greatest buildings in the country, they belong, of course, not so much to the parish with its strong homely sentiment as to the whole nation, and that in a way without parallel in Europe.

The cathedral is the Bishop's church; and in England the Reformation in no way diminished the importance of the Bishop. The break with Rome made him the representative of a national church, one of the representatives of the whole nation: and owing to that he still keeps a political importance he has lost long ago in other countries. The Bishop has a seat in the House of Lords.* It is still his acknowledged right to give expression in Parliament to the national conscience. He is a great dignitary surrounded with a princely retinue of clerics, and

* When the great increase of the population in the nineteenth century led to the creation of new dioceses, the number of Bishops with a seat in the Lords was reduced to thirty.

the way in which the stalls and the Bishop's throne are arranged in the choir reminds one in every cathedral of this imposing hierarchy and the princely rank of the bearer of the crozier. Most of the English cathedrals have the character of abbey churches. The cathedral is not intimately surrounded by the older houses of the city, as it would be in France or Germany: it is the centre, as it were, of its own manor, complete with cloisters, Bishop's Palace and other buildings, and a greensward with old trees, like a park, puts a distance between the buildings and the worldly bustle of the city. Only two of the cathedrals illustrated in this book, Peterborough and Gloucester, were actually founded as conventual churches—to be raised later on (under Henry VIII) to cathedral status. All the others were built by Bishops as the principal churches of their diocese, whether the cathedral clergy lived under the monastic discipline of the Benedictine rule, as in Canterbury, Winchester, Durham, Ely, Worcester, and Rochester, or whether they were secular clergy as at York, Lincoln, Lichfield, Hereford, Wells, Salisbury, and Exeter. The cloisters and the other characteristics of the conventual church, in particular its strict division into a church for the congregation in the nave and a church in the choir for the clergy, indicate here in England not so much monastic seclusion as the division in the State between clerisy and laity.

Travel along the straight highways over the flats of northern France, where the open fields stretch away on either side. Step into one of those prodigious Gothic cathedrals the majestic dignity of whose towers dominate the countryside: your eyes at once take in the whole solemn interior; the pillars and the vaulting of the nave are completed mystically and harmoniously in the glow of the many-coloured windows of the choir. Even the view down the transepts to the scintillation of their own rose-windows only fulfils that one impression of greatness even more.

But in England, in this green island, the ancient road winds away over range after gentle range of hills which keep shutting out the view and opening it up afresh, the road leads through a landscape like a park, made up of fields and pastures enclosed between hedges and stone walls and parcelled out between bush, and tree and copse. You come to a cathedral which in its majesty commands one of the wide hollows, or as at Lincoln and Durham stands enthroned high over the city: you go inside, you see at first only the nave. You look east and under the intersection of the transepts the nave is cut off by the screen, in which the organ is sometimes placed; and where an old screen has not been preserved, you can be sure that Sir George Gilbert Scott, the Viollet-le-Duc of English cathedrals in the nineteenth century, will have built a new one. At the point where transepts and nave intersect, the style often changes all of a sudden from Norman to Gothic, in Winchester from the Gothic of the nave to the almost suffocating sternness and weight of the early Norman pillars and arches. Behind the screen opens the choir, a cathedral in itself with a series of separate creations of space, such as the altar space or the presbytery, the ambulatory and its chapels, sometimes separated from one another by more screens and running beyond the retrochoir until they end in the Lady-chapel built out to the east. Usually these spaces grouped together east of the screen stretch for a longer distance than the whole of the nave. But if you stand under the crossing and look up, you enjoy yet another spatial experience. The central tower rises up like a cathedral within a cathedral illuminated by the arcaded windows all around and ending in the finest timbered vaulting (Canterbury, York). At Ely, where the tremendous pillars of the crossing spread out fanwise to carry the glory of the lantern, this is developed in the grandest way into a new notion of space. Outside the church the sequence of spatial units, even more distinct from each other, is continued in the subsidiary chapels, the chapter-house, and cloister; and, down below, in the crypts, which survive mostly from the earliest periods of building.

*

The conversion of England was due in the main to St. Augustine (from 596), and so the building of churches began; but architecture in this island needed a stronger impulse to make it blossom into creativity.

The erection of immense cathedrals began immediately after Duke William the Norman had gained the throne by his victory at Hastings in 1066. Of the pre-Norman cathedrals hardly anything is left. The Romanesque style had been used in England before the Conquest, but it had never provoked a desire to build with any greatness of character. With William there now came to the Bishops' thrones that band of forceful personalities who in the next century gave a Norman-French stamp to the church in England. Far into the Gothic era we find French names, and for a long while the inscriptions on the tombs (when they are not in Latin) remain French; many years had to pass before the English language could penetrate into the church. As master-builders the Norman bishops brought with them a grand concept of the union of spiritual and temporal power. This was maintained as a strong tradition, and gradually the daring spirit of the Normans mingled with the tenaciously conservative spirit of the Anglo-Saxons—a synthesis heralded in that Early Gothic which is rightly called "Early English".

In Canterbury, Archbishop Lanfranc of Caen laid the foundation stone of his new cathedral in 1070, about 1080 Archbishop Thomas of Bayeux followed his example in York, Bishop Warrelwast, a nephew of the Conqueror, built a new church at Exeter, in Winchester a cathedral arose under Bishop Walkelin between 1079 and 1093, the year of its consecration, at Rochester Bishop Gundulf pulled down the Anglo-Saxon fabric in 1080 to make room for a more magnificent church which was to house his Benedictines, at St. Albans Abbot Paul of Caen began to rebuild between 1077 and 1080, Abbot Simeon of Ely started rebuilding in 1080, and was followed in 1089 by the first Norman Abbot of Gloucester and in 1118 by Abbot John of Sais at Peterborough. William of St. Carileph founded the huge cathedral at Durham in 1093. Norwich became a see in 1094 and two years later Herbert of Losinga laid the first stone of his Norman and Benedictine cathedral. Bishop Wulfstan of Worcester, the only Anglo-Saxon to keep his bishopric after the Conquest, played his part from 1084 in this noble architectural competition.

So these massive Norman buildings which reflect the spirit of the Conqueror came into being, some of them to be finished only in the course of centuries—these buildings characterized by the round Norman arch and the zigzag ornament, which we find again on the other side of the Channel and wherever the Normans ruled, right down to Sicily. The wide bulk of the cathedral is usually dominated by the lofty central tower, the ceilings are flat, and made of wood, and painted (the nave of Durham, with its arcade of immense pillars, a true citadel of the Grail, was rib-vaulted in stone before 1133).

The Norman style of Romanesque predominated till late in the twelfth century, when in France the Gothic principle had already been established. The ornament became more and more luxuriant and extensive, and the painting of the plastered wall surfaces of the interior, added to the richly interlaced decoration of the stonework (in which the old Celtic ornamentation was still active), produced an impression of the utmost splendour. The interiors became more and more immense, rising at Peterborough and above all at Ely to a height of delicacy and daring which no later Gothic interior in the country ever rivalled. The façades of Lincoln and Ely are wilful in their grandeur: holding fast to the Norman arch, they violently enlarge the scale of the Romanesque.

Although one speaks in England of a special transitional style, Gothic established itself more suddenly and later than in France, becoming, it is true, more and more the peculiar national style of England. Once more the decisive impulse came from continental Europe; when in Canterbury, four years after the murder of Thomas à Becket, Prior Conrad's celebrated choir was burnt down in 1174, the rebuilding was entrusted to William of Sens, who brought over to England the Early Gothic style of Burgundy ready-made. English scholars point out that, almost simultaneously and independently elsewhere, as at Wells, the English created a native school of architecture in this new language of form. In 1178 William of Sens fell from the scaffolding as he was superintending the work at Canterbury. The crippled master-builder supervised the completion of the east transept from his bed, and then handed over to William the Englishman.

English Gothic is divided into three epochs: Early English from about 1175 to 1250, corresponding to Early Gothic, Decorated from about 1250 to 1340, corresponding to High Gothic, and Perpendicular (or Late Gothic) after 1340. From Norman times the broad disposition of the mass and the strong accentuation of the crossing were retained almost everywhere, the vertical always being subdued by the horizontal. The "classic" façade of the French cathedral, the dominating porches so richly ornamented with statuary and crowned with rose-windows and galleries and towers—none of this was widely accepted in England. The English porches play only a minor part in the surface pattern of the west front. The *Biblia pauperum*, the Bibles of the Poor, full of crowned figures out of English or Old Testament history, spread in a single pattern between vertical and horizontal bands right up to the towers (at Salisbury and Lichfield the figures have been renewed, at Wells alone the original work remains in its richness, at Exeter the figures, now much decayed, are crowded together on the low story between the porch and the deep recession of the west window). In the arrangement too of the Gothic interior "English wilfulness speaks, in comparison with the classic of the Continent, in remarkable contrasts" (K. Escher). More and more the architectural problem gave wings to the imagination of the native masters and carried them to independent solutions: after the choir at Canterbury, which introduces the pointed arch into England, two other choirs mark the most important stages in development. These are the splendidly lit Angel Choir at Lincoln (1255–1288), the early climax of the Decorated style, its decoration culminating in the figures of angels in the triforium, and the choir at Gloucester (1337–1377). The immense luminous east window at Gloucester and the almost excessive richness of the starry vault decorated with its angelic musicians, magnificently sound the first notes of the Perpendicular. In the cloister of the same cathedral in 1370 one of the richest of fan-vaults was built, foreshadowed in the centrally planned structure of the chapter-house which spreads out from the column in the middle like the leaves of a palm tree.

The sculpture in the English cathedrals (except for a few of the tombs) cannot be compared with the greatest achievements of the same kind on the Continent. Even the imposing number of royal statues in their intense and solemn attitude on the front at Wells can hardly be measured against the masterpieces around the porches at Chartres, Rheims, and Amiens. It was in ornamental decoration, in the foliage of the capitals and corbels that the English stone-carver in the High Gothic found his full aesthetic freedom. His decorative imagination could now even affect the development of ecclesiastical architecture abroad: without the English Gothic the French Flamboyant style is scarcely conceivable.

The fourteenth century brought with it no great building schemes like those of the early bishops, but it allowed the national Gothic to spread through the country. The splendid example of cathedral architecture was followed in the town churches and the country churches in castles and in town houses, and it has lived its tenacious life right up to our own day. The Tudor period continued the Gothic, and the Romantic period was able to blend with the elements of romance that habit (which from the very beginning was inherent in English Gothic) of masking space so as to predict still more space, that unsuspected succession of new experience after experience. In the nineteenth century Gothic buildings still went up in England—for example that representative building of the nation, the House of Commons, which exerts a more genuine effect than most of the architecture of the same period on the Continent. And it was through his passionate understanding of Gothic that William Morris was able to revive arts and crafts, and especially typography, and able also to re-inspire politics by insisting on the unity of idea, and individual man, and labour.

As we look at them today, the cathedrals are to some extent the product of nineteenth-century restoration; the restorers compromised between their own view of the history of art and the liturgical requirements of the Anglican Church now stirred to new life, they tried to arrest the decay of the fabric and to make good the disfiguring damage done during the Reformation and the Enlightenment. It is due to the accidents of history that today we are more familiar with the names of these revivalists than we are with the names of the medieval architects whose creations, so rich, so imaginative, have often come down to us as if they were no more than the anonymous expression of a remarkable community of experience.* The activities of the architect James Wyatt (1748–1813; from 1796 he was surveyor-general to the Board of Works) must be considered calamitous. He restored a number of cathedrals, Salisbury and Lichfield especially, in the Neo-Classical spirit, and was given the title of "The Destroyer" by those who were more intimate with the nature of Gothic. It was chiefly due to John Carter, his descriptions, engravings and plans, which he carried out partly for the Society of Antiquaries, that the architecture of cathedrals in the Middle Ages became better understood. In the mid-nineteenth century the Gothic style triumphed in new churches, monuments and other public buildings, and the architects now felt they must make the old cathedrals "correct": they were not content only to restore the fabric in an understanding way, they had to replace the lost sculpture (for instance on the great façades of Salisbury and Lichfield), they had to replace the choir stalls and the windows, they believed they must continue the work of the medieval master-builders by introducing new screens and other trimmings. All this is represented best in the man who designed the Albert Memorial, Sir George Gilbert Scott (1811–1878), himself the son and the grandson of a clergyman. His own grandchild is that Sir Giles Gilbert Scott, who since 1904 has been building a vast new cathedral at Liverpool in a pure Gothic manner—something which could only be undertaken now in England where there is such a wealth of tradition and where the Gothic achievement has been so constant and persistent.

*

The English cathedrals have their own atmosphere. They are not Catholic, and they are not Protestant—as they are, one way or the other, abroad. You do not first have to fetch the key, when you want to visit them on a weekday, as you do in visiting the Reformed churches on the Continent; they are open from morning to dusk, and nearly always there are visitors pacing up and down—particularly old ladies—busily reading in their guide-books. The verger and his assistants in their black robes pay strict attention to propriety and tidiness and take care that the services are not disturbed. Even on a weekday, from the light carillons which suggest the south of Europe to the deep booming tenors, the cathedral bells call the devout to prayer at least three times. Even now the constant sound of bells and the host of visitors make a small cathedral city like Wells seem a centre of pilgrimage. Splendid bunches of flowers stand in tall vases on floor and altar, constantly renewed with exquisite taste. But in this tidiness you

* In his *Gothic England: A Survey of National Culture* (London 1947) John Harvey has emphasized in a passionate and personal manner the importance of the great individuals and individual achievements in medieval architecture.

miss the smell of incense, which the cold pillars themselves in the continental churches seem to exhale, you miss the glimmer of candles in front of statues of the Virgin in the dark side aisles, and all that mysterious atmosphere of Catholic places of worship which despite their modern gimcrackery and bad taste take one right back into the world of the Gothic and Romanesque builders.

*

A word about the photographs in this book. Reverence for the subject seemed to us to demand that the architecture should be reproduced accurately and that all effects of unnatural perspective or lighting should be avoided. We have made no use of the exaggerations of a wide-angled lens. They are often the only way of showing an interior completely, but they distort the proportions and give a false impression. In order to give a general idea of seventeen of the most important English cathedrals we had to limit the number of photographs of each one (though some of them deserve a whole book of this size). For the sake of variety, we have not repeated the orthodox views, frontal and entire, of each cathedral, however important these may be for historical comparison. We have tried instead to add to the wealth of existing illustration by taking new photographs of detail, aiming to show, in particular, the rich fancy of the English vaulting. We were tempted to include the rather important sculpture of the monuments, but this would have spoilt the unity of our theme and limited our choice still more. The photographs show a number of not very inspiring fixtures for electric light, wires, chairs, loudspeakers, scaffolding, and some windows which have still to be completely repaired after the war. These objects could not be avoided and we ask indulgence for them. They are part of the impression received by visitors today, a part, it is to be hoped, the reader will overlook when faced with the majesty and beauty of these daring towers, façades, and interiors.

CANTERBURY (Kent), Christ-Church Cathedral

Plate 1. Air photograph (Aerofilms)
Plate 9. From Britton's *Cathedral Antiquities*
Photographs, Plates 14–22

In 597 Pope Gregory the Great sent the Benedictine monk Augustinus, the Apostle of the Anglo-Saxons, to Cantawarabyrig, the "town of the men of Kent" and capital of King Ethelbert. Here Augustine introduced Christianity and founded the first English bishopric. Since then Canterbury has been the seat of the primate of England. After the murder of Archbishop Thomas à Becket in 1170, the cathedral became the most famous centre of pilgrimage in the country. As primate of all England, the Archbishop of Canterbury at the Reformation became head of the Church of England.

St. Augustine's Romano-British church was rebuilt in 950 by Archbishop Odo, and the new cathedral was burnt down in 1067, just after the Norman Conquest. The building we have today was begun in the same year by the Lombard, Archbishop Lanfranc, the friend of William the Conqueror (whose north-west tower was pulled down as late as 1834). It is a rambling complication of Romanesque and Early and Late Gothic. The work was carried on under Archbishop Anselm (1093–1109) by the prior Ernulph (1096–1107). They replaced the earlier choir (which, with its three apses, adjoined the western transept) with a new choir stretching far to the east, and they crossed it with a second transept. Each wing of this additional transept was given two small apses on the eastern side. Round the choir stretched an ambulatory, and a chapel was built out on either side of it at a tangent. Another chapel was added beyond the ambulatory at the far end of the cathedral. All of this, a work famous for its splendour, was completed by Prior Conrad (1108–1126) and consecrated in 1130. A good deal remains, the whole of the crypt, the lower stories of the two east towers and of the outer walling of the side-aisles of the choir, and also the eastern transept, complete with its two staircase turrets, and the two chapels joining the ambulatory. There survive as well an unusual number of monastic buildings of every kind, which are Late Romanesque.

This second choir was burnt down in 1174. Master William of Sens (from France) began to rebuild a year later with stone shipped across the Channel from Caen in Normandy. In 1178 he had a fall from the scaffolding and was succeeded by William the Englishman (1179–1184). The Romanesque eastern transept and the outer walls of the choir were retained, except for the end wall. But this entailed a number of unusual compromises. For example, the central aisle had to be narrowed and bent inwards on the site of the end wall of the old choir (Plate 20). The two triforium-like blind arcades, one above the other, in the wings of the eastern transept, result from incorporating the older Romanesque windows in the new Gothic structure (Plate 21). Round arches and pointed arches are used together.

The vaulting of the eastern transept and the altar space was completed in 1179; and from the altar space the choir narrows into Trinity Chapel and continues, until at last it opens into the circular east chapel. This chapel, the "Corona" or "Becket's Crown", housed an altar containing a fragment of St. Thomas à Becket's skull. It was vaulted in 1184. The crypt was much extended at the same time (Plate 19).

The rebuilding of the nave and of the western transept on the Romanesque foundations began in 1378 under Archbishop Simon of Sudbury (1375–1381) and was carried out under Prior Chillenden (1390–1411). Magnificent in its proportions, this new work is one of the early examples of the Late Gothic style in its full development (Plates 15–17). At the same time the piers of the crossing were strengthened by bridges of stone tracery spanning all four arches (Plate 17), and the stone choir-screen (Plate 18) was added. The central tower, or "Angel Steeple", with its fine fan-vaulting, was erected between 1495 and 1503 by Prior Goldstone (Plate 22). The ground-plan also shows the two rectangular chapels, each of them set slightly at an angle, on the east side of the wings of the western transept. The one on the north is the Lady-chapel. It was in the transept alongside this chapel that Becket was murdered. The rectangular treasury is reached through the northern chapel of the ambulatory. The great cloister occupies an unusual position on the north side, with a rectangular chapter-house and beside it on the left the library. From here and from the east transept is the entrance to a Late Romanesque water-tower (baptistry), joined on the east by a library room. There are also extensive remains of Romanesque and Gothic buildings.

I

General view from the air.

9

"Becket's Crown", the circular chapel added behind the choir by William the Englishman, who also built the Trinity Chapel, for the relics of St. Thomas à Becket (from Britton's *Cathedral Antiquities*, 1821). It was finished in 1184. The altar with the relics of St. Thomas à Becket no longer exists but the chapel contains the ancient "Chair of St. Augustine" used at the installation of the Archbishop. Here and in the ambulatory there is stained glass of the thirteenth and fourteenth centuries. The marble throne was placed here later. The chapel is a pure example (and one of the earlier examples) of the Early English style.

14

View from the south-west. In the centre stands the "Angel Steeple" of 1495–1503. The tower-like building on the extreme right is "Becket's Crown".

15

The Late Gothic nave, begun in 1378. On the left is the south tower of the west façade, on the right the great window of the south wing of the western transept, in Perpendicular style, stressing the upright movement in the tracery.

16

From the south-west. The nave on the left (as in Plate 15). Notice the special beauty of the strong, simple buttresses. The central tower, or "Angel Steeple" (1495–1503) is one of the most beautiful in England (for the interior vaulting, see Plate 22). To the right of the tower projects the southern wing of the western transept, and farther to the right (behind the foliage) is the southern wing of the eastern transept, its lower story Romanesque, its upper story Early Gothic.

17

The nave, begun in 1373. This is one of the noblest, most complete, and most restful spatial compositions of the Perpendicular style. The perfect organization of pillars, walls, and lierne vault, give a like feeling of harmony. To the east, the pillars are buttressed by the bridges of pierced tracery in the crossing arches (for a more powerful solution of the same problem compare Plates 65, 91, and 94). Notice the rich stone screen dating from 1390 to 1411, in the time of Prior Chillenden (compare Plate 18); and beyond the crossing the light, simple, sexpartite vault of the choir, which is Early Gothic.

18

Choir screen, 1400. This is partly modelled on an older one of 1304, and is therefore rather Decorated than Perpendicular. Under the very ornate canopies are statues of Henry V, Richard II, and Ethelbert.

19

The crypt below the end of the choir (Plate 20), with a view cast into the crypt below "Becket's Crown". The shafts of the slim pillars, the moulded capitals of the massive cylindrical piers, and the ribs are made of the black polished marble from the Purbeck quarries.

20

The eastern end of the choir, the Trinity Chapel, built between 1179 and 1184 by William the Englishman, probably after the plans of William of Sens. This may be the first appearance in England of the true Early Gothic. The stone was transported by sea from Caen in Normandy. Suitable quarries in the south of England were only discovered later. The coupled cylindrical pillars in the foreground and in the Trinity Chapel were modelled on pillars in the cathedral of Sens, to which there are other resemblances. The nearest pillars stand on the foundations of the end of the Romanesque choir. Evidently the lengthening of the choir was only decided upon at this point. The indecision has disturbed the spatial effect. The dark shafts of the thin piers of the vault are again of black Purbeck marble. So are the small columns of the gallery arcade (the "triforium", not an actual gallery, but the articulation of the wall space, on the outside of which the steep roof meets the side-aisles). The sharply carved ornamentation of the ribs and cornices is what is known in England as "dog-tooth". A passage was cut out of the thickness of the wall below the clerestory windows, as in the earlier Norman-Romanesque building. The rich shrine for the bones of St. Thomas à Becket, placed inside

Ground-plan of Canterbury Cathedral
(from *The Builder*, 1891)

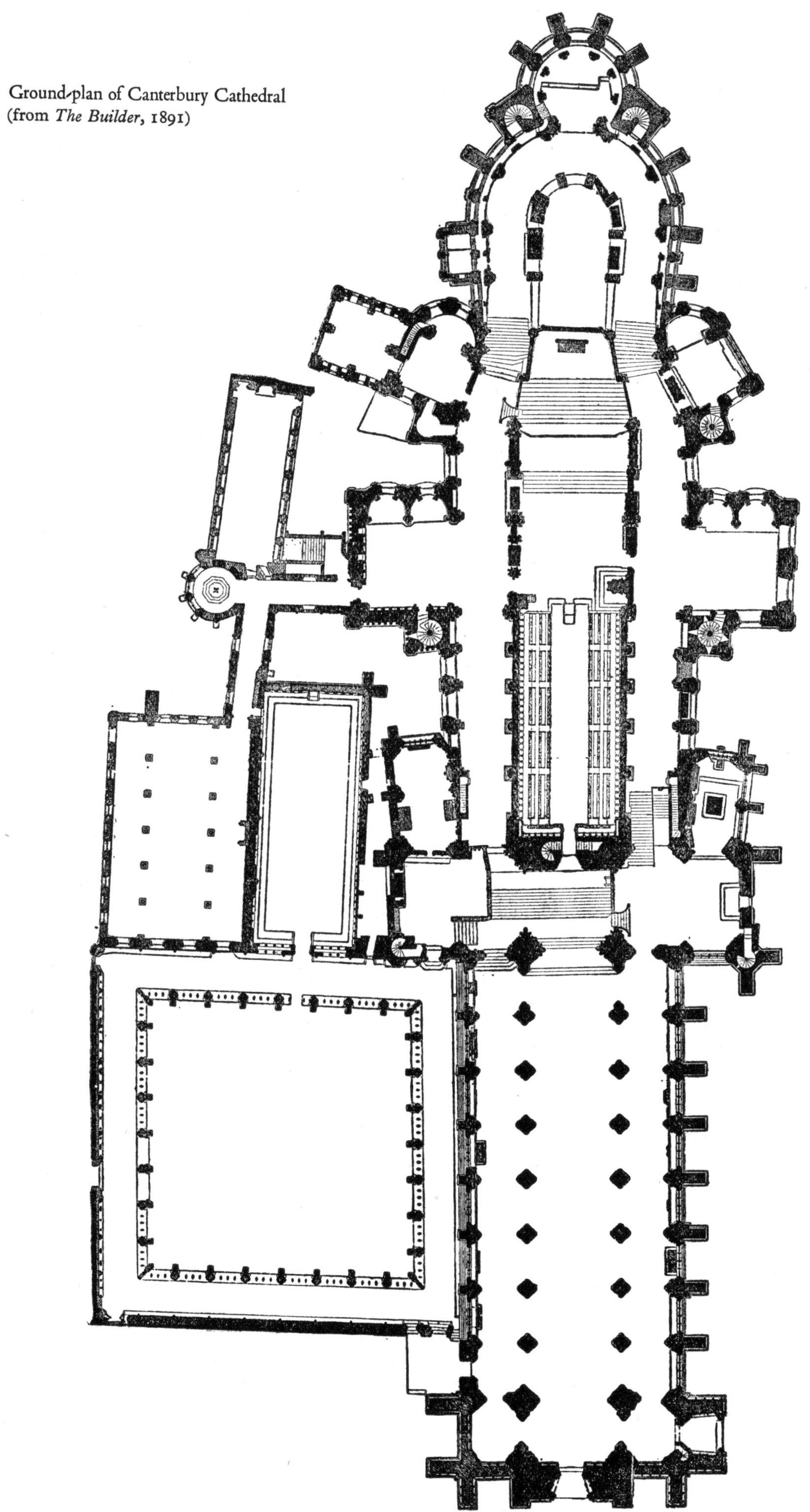

Trinity Chapel in 1220, was plundered and destroyed by Henry VIII in 1538. The numerous tombs and burial chapels in the choir are mostly Late Gothic.

21

The northern wing of the eastern transept. The walls are Romanesque, refashioned in the Gothic style by William of Sens and vaulted between 1178 and 1184. The vaulting is sexpartite. Two arcades, one above the other, take in the Romanesque windows.

22

The western crossing, with a view of the fan-vaulting in the "Angel Steeple" (1495–1503). These fan-vaults (compare Plates 52, 109, 110, and for the earlier form Plates 58, 60, 62, 65, 78, 119) are a specifically English invention, developed out of the multiplication of the lierne ribs. There is nothing comparable on the Continent, though the much simpler stone vaulting in buildings of the Teutonic Knights in East Prussia was inspired by English examples.

ROCHESTER (Kent), St. Andrew's Cathedral

Plates 23–27

In 604 St. Augustine consecrated the first bishop of Rochester. The cathedral was destroyed at the Conquest, and in 1082 Gandulph, the second Norman bishop, began a new building. He replaced the lay-priests of Rochester with Benedictine monks.

Rochester is one of the smallest abbey-cathedrals. It follows the usual plan of a larger western transept for the lay congregation, and a smaller eastern transept between the actual choir, containing the choir stalls, and the east choir with the high altar, known as the "presbyterium".

Not much is left of the Early Romanesque cathedral of Bishop Gandulph. The five-aisled west crypt dates probably from an extension under Ernulf between 1115 and 1124. The well-preserved Romanesque nave was built between 1140 and 1150. Its more or less large size gives it a spatial effect which is powerful and almost archaic, and this is much intensified by the sturdy open roof (although this wooden roof is Late Gothic). Each pier of the arcade is different. Each is topped with a low capital like a cornice, and from the capitals rise simply constructed arches, the voussoirs of which are ornamented with zigzag pattern. The voussoirs of the gallery arcade above are ornamented in the same way. But there was never, it seems, a real gallery, and the double arches open rather into the side-aisles. The arches act merely as a bridge from pillar to pillar. There are examples of a similar arrangement in Romanesque and Gothic churches in France. The voussoirs of the gallery arcade are in part richly decorated with diaper work, which in France is called "gauffrure", in Germany "Waffelmuster". And the thick walls are pierced throughout their length, and on a level with the top of the arcade, by a passage, and are thus divided into two. It is a typical Norman method taken over by the Gothic. The façade is Late Romanesque of about 1160. Of the chapter-house built at this time only the east wall is left; and there are traces of the cloister.

Of the Gothic portions, the pillars of the crossing were rebuilt between 1179 and 1200, the piers having shafts of black Purbeck marble. The upper choir, the eastern transept, and the presbytery were rebuilt in the days of Bishop William de Hov (1201–1227); and the presbytery with its mighty Purbeck shafts is a perfect sample of Early English, the regional form in England of Early Gothic. Underneath, the enlargement of the crypt explains the considerable difference in the levels of choir and nave. The western transept was built between 1240 and 1255, the north wing first. The south wing has ribbed vaulting of wood. In 1280–1313 the two eastern bays of the nave next to the crossing were replaced with higher Gothic arches, and the tribune was done away with. The tower over the crossing was built in 1393. The Lady-chapel has an unusual position in the angle between the southern wing of the transept and the nave (Plate 23).

23

Rochester from the south-west, seen from the keep of the old Norman castle of the city. On the right in front of the transept is the Lady-chapel, built in 1500.

CANTERBURY 1

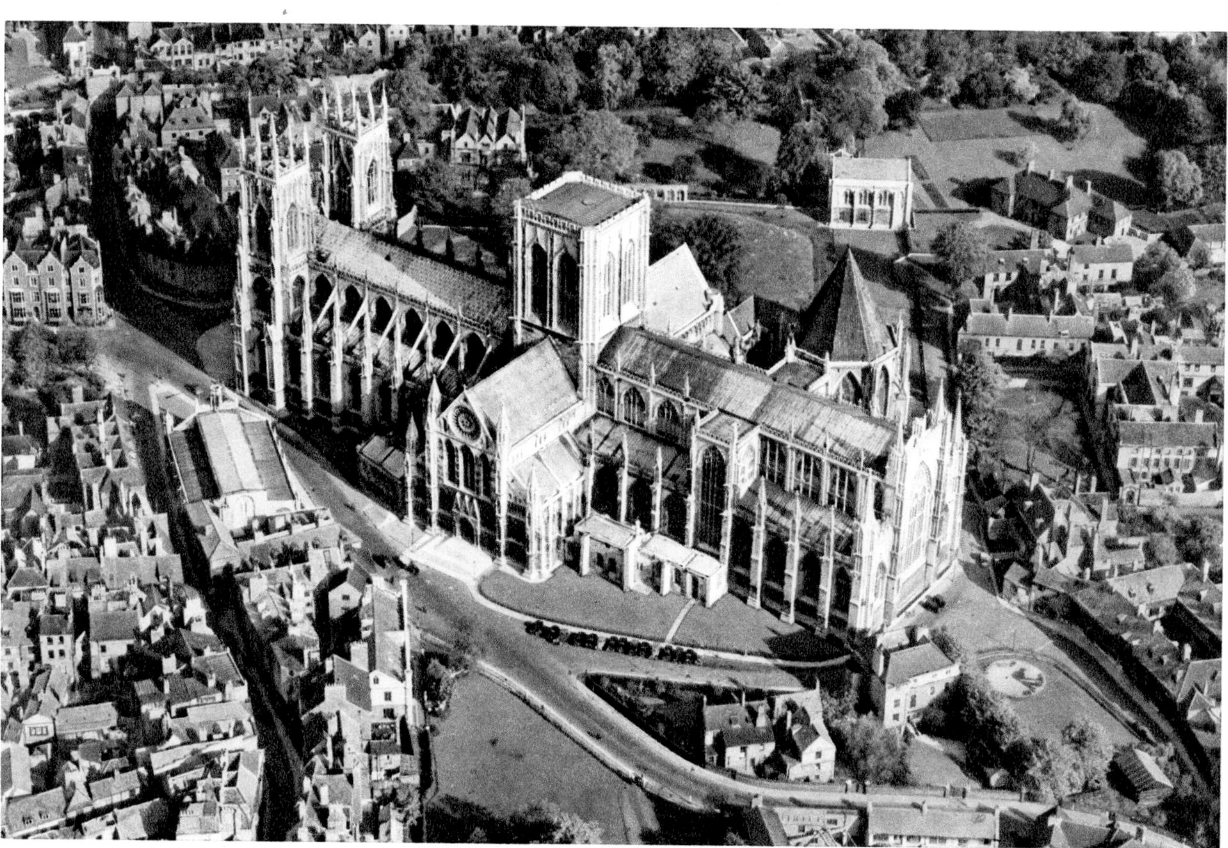

YORK 2

GLOUCESTER 3

WINCHESTER 4

WELLS 5

EXETER 6

NORWICH 7

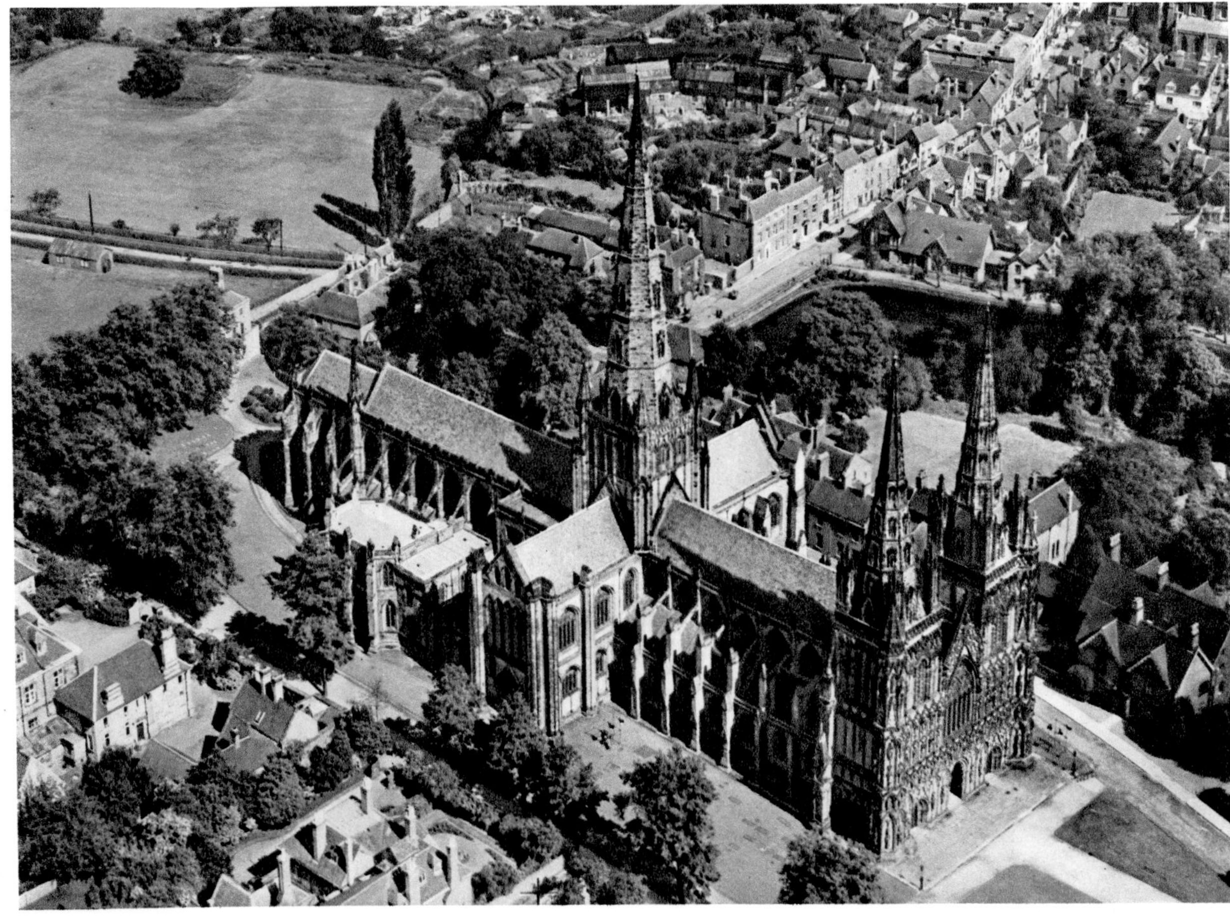

LICHFIELD 8

The outer turrets of the side-aisles stand higher than was originally intended.

24

The Late Romanesque façade, of about 1160. The west window and the crenellated gable are Late Gothic of the fifteenth century. The door jambs are carved with figures after French prototypes. Christ sits in Glory in the tympanum. Compare this Late Romanesque richness with the façade at Ely (Plate 34).

25

The nave looking east to the crossing, with the choir behind, and immediately in front the two eastern bays of the nave replaced in the Gothic style between 1280 and 1313. The rood-screen is modern.

26, 27

The eastern part of the extended crypt, built when the choir was enlarged under Bishop William de Hov (1201–1227).

ST. ALBANS (Hertfordshire), St. Alban's Cathedral

Plates 28–32

THE Benedictine abbey of St. Alban was founded in 793 in honour of England's first martyr, the Roman soldier Alban, who was put to death under the Emperor Diocletian. In the Middle Ages it was one of the richest and most powerful monasteries in England. The abbey-church was built by Abbot Paul of Caen, with the help of Archbishop Lanfranc. After the Reformation it became a parish church in 1550, and was raised to a cathedral only in 1877. This imposing church is the chief example of the Early Romanesque style in England. In contrast to the cathedrals at Ely and Peterborough, it shows only an even progression of plain surfaces and almost no plastic articulation. The wooden ceiling is modern, a weak version of Late Gothic. But because of it St. Alban's must have more of its original look than other churches whose early wooden ceilings were replaced later in the Middle Ages.

The church was consecrated in 1115. In Abbot Paul's nave, built between 1077 and 1088, there are only ten bays, but the great length is due to the giant piers which are almost as wide as the arches. On the north side the nave keeps its original form (except for the four most westerly bays). The three bays nearest the crossing on the south side, the transept (with a few alterations), and the strong, fortress-like tower over the crossing are also original. These are all made of smooth Roman brick from the old Roman city of St. Albans (Verulamium), plastered over, and with many fragments of Romanesque and Gothic wall-painting. In the arcaded openings of the transept small pillars from an Anglo-Saxon building have been used again in an adapted form.

The Gothic west façade in freestone was begun by Bishop John de Cella (1195–1214), but except for the porches it was rebuilt in the nineteenth century. Bishop William of Trumpington (1212–1235) renewed four arches of the north and five of the south side of the nave in the Gothic style, and John of Hertford (1235–1260) demolished the Romanesque choir and built a new Gothic choir of greater length. In 1323 a partial collapse in the Romanesque arcading on the south side of the nave made it necessary to rebuild the five bays next to the crossing. The windows of the northern side-aisle date from about 1400, the windows and vaulting in the side-aisle on the south are work of the late nineteenth century. The monastery buildings, except for a Late Gothic gateway, were all destroyed when the abbey was dissolved at the Reformation.

28

The nave, the south wing of the transept, and the central tower from the south-west. The transept and the tower are Romanesque and were built of Roman brick (so were the three adjoining bays inside the nave: the five bays next to them were renewed after 1323 and the Gothic bays were built between 1214 and 1235).

29

The nave, looking eastward. In the left foreground the first of the four Gothic arches, then the original piers and arches of the Norman building. In the foreground, right, the arcade of 1214–1235. And beyond the Romanesque pilaster the five bays built after 1323. The three Romanesque bays are hidden by the organ.

30

The central tower from the north-east. On the right, the north wing of the transept. On the left, the western portion of the choir.

31

The north side of the nave. Note the impressive Norman architecture, the piers of plastered brick, the (mainly Gothic) wall-paintings. The first of the four Gothic western bays comes outside the picture on the extreme left.

32

View through the crossing from the south wing into the north wing of the transept. In the gallery arcade above, on the left, can be seen the older Anglo-Saxon columns which the Norman builders used a second time. On the right, at the top, is the passage cut through the thickness of the wall. The voussoirs of the arches in the crossing are coloured alternately in stone and brick. The open tower rises over the crossing; and the outer wall of the northern wing of the Romanesque transept is pierced with an Early Gothic rose-window.

ELY (Cambridgeshire), Cathedral of the Holy Trinity

Plates 33–45

ELY is a Benedictine foundation of the seventh century which can be traced back to St. Etheldreda, Queen of Northumberland, who founded the abbey in 673. The huge, towery mass of the Norman abbey-cathedral is placed romantically on the Isle of Ely, a hill among he low-lying fens. It was one of the last strongholds of the Anglo-Saxons and was not surrendered to the Conqueror until 1071. The first of the Norman abbots, Abbot Simeon (1081–1093), brother of Abbot Walkelin of Winchester, began to build, or rebuild, in 1083. The eastern part was finished when Ely became a bishop's seat in 1109. Today, the oldest portions are the arcades of the transept. In the sides of the transept there were originally open galleries, as there are still at Winchester (dotted lines on ground-plan, cf. Plate 63). The nave was finished in 1180. The western transept, immediately behind the west front or façade, lacks its northern wing and was never finished. It forms a kind of vestibule, though a chapel (restored) was added to the south wing of the transept on the eastern side. This uncompleted transept dates probably from the third quarter of the twelfth century. The pillars of the western crossing were strengthened in 1380; and as a result the vestibule is cut off from the nave even more than it was originally (Plate 38). The splendid west tower articulated entirely in openings and niches exemplifies Late Romanesque in its last phase. So does the whole of the west front, interspersed with pointed lancets tending towards the Gothic. The motive of the lance-like shafts which span the wall is carried over the surface (Plates 33, 34). The western tower and façade date from about 1200. The crowning octagon of the tower was built probably about 1400, and until 1757 it was surmounted by a leaded spire.

After Peterborough, Ely is the outstanding monument of the mature Norman style, in which the walls are plastically articulated. Here too, although restored, the wooden roof survives in the Norman, or Romanesque, part of the building.

Ely is also rich in Gothic. The finely designed structure in front of the west tower, the Galilee, was added under Bishop Eustace (1197–1215). The smooth transition from Late Romanesque to Early Gothic is well shown in Plates 33 and 34. The Romanesque choir was demolished by Bishop Hugh of Northwold (1229–1254), and the presbytery was rebuilt, the present six eastern bays after 1234. This, and the Angel Choir of Lincoln, are the richest examples of English Early Gothic on the brink of the Decorated style. The shafts are Purbeck marble. The moulding of the arches is carved into dogtooth or foliage; and the choir terminates as usual in a straight east wall.

In 1322 the central tower collapsed, in the time of Bishop John Hotham (1316–1337). It was boldly decided to contrive an octagonal space to the full width of the nave (including the side-aisles) and to do away with the old pillars. This Octagon is unique in Gothic architecture, and it was finished in 1342 under

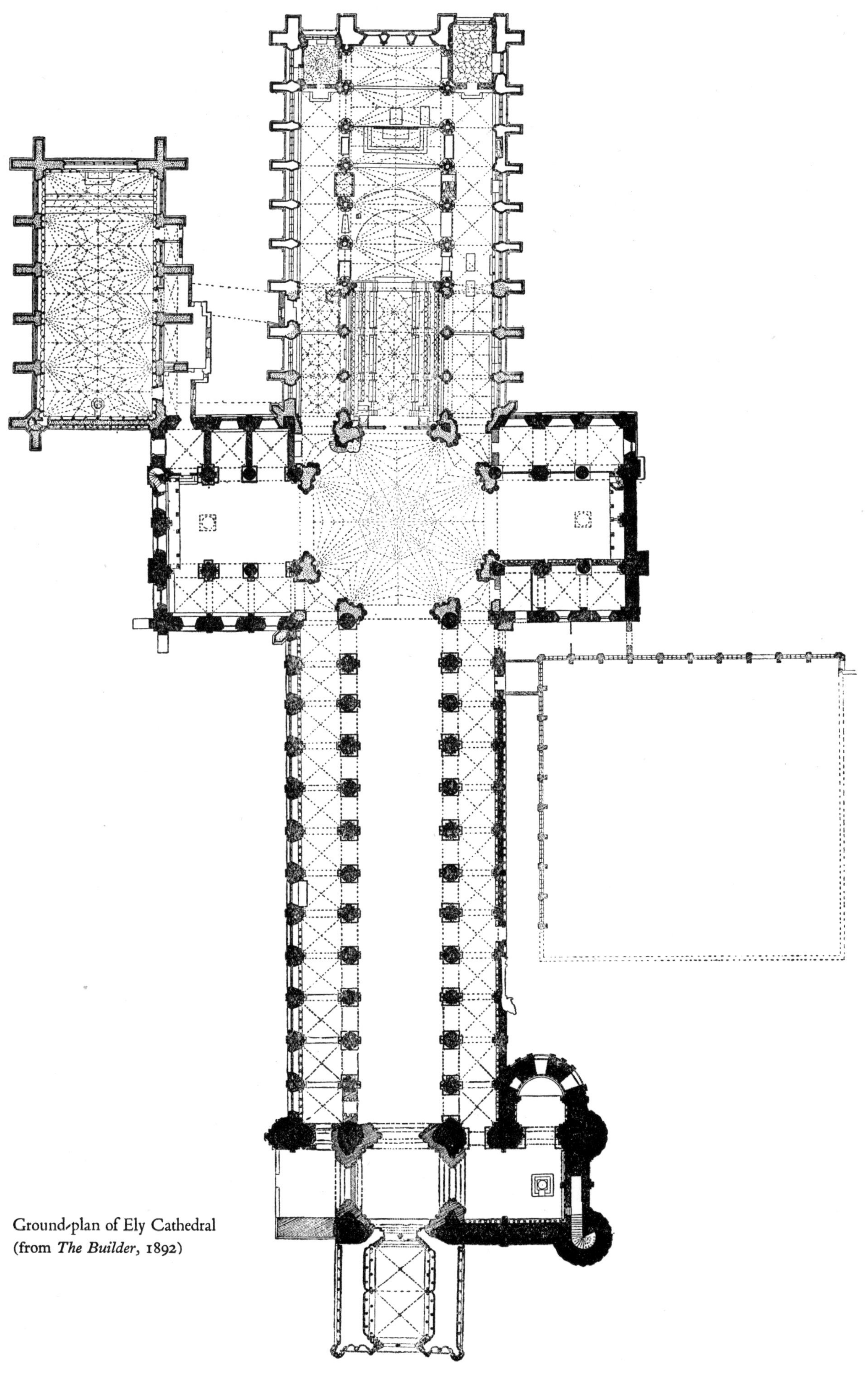

Ground-plan of Ely Cathedral
(from *The Builder*, 1892)

the direction of the sacrist of the church, Alan of Walsingham. The rib-vaulting above the Octagon, and the lantern which it supports, are both made of wood. The three western bays of the choir, which were also destroyed when the tower fell, were rebuilt at the same time in the richest Decorated style. Contrary to custom, the Lady-chapel is a separate building, which stands parallel with the choir at the east corner of the northern wing of the transept. It is a rectangle without side-aisles, with five bays on each side. Built between 1321 and 1349 by Brother John Wisbeck, it is one of the richest and most graceful interiors of its period, a stage further towards Late Gothic than continental work of the same time. In the choir there are several chantry chapels: Bishop Alcock's chantry at the north-east corner, Bishop West's at the south-east, and between them the east bay of the centre aisle which serves as a Lady-chapel. There are many other chapels and tombs between the choir arches. Over on the right there are remains of the cloister.

33

The west façade, and the transept with one wing complete, the other not completed. The unfinished transept with the two towers or turrets dates from the third quarter of the twelfth century, the west tower from about 1200, and the octagonal crown of the tower from about 1400. The Early Gothic Galilee projecting in front of the tower was built between 1200 and 1215.

34

The outer wall between the western towers, executed with the extreme richness of the later phase of Romanesque. Much of the surface glimmers with diaper work, the arches are carved with dogtooth and with lozenge ornament in the mouldings. The richness of the design conceals a certain insignificance. On the left is the south wall of the Galilee.

35

The "Prior's Door", a Romanesque doorway from the south aisle into the cloister (which no longer exists). In the tympanum Christ is enthroned in Glory, supported by angels. The surface ornament, twisting about and richly diversified, is typical of a somewhat barbaric opulence.

36

The "Monks' Door", a Romanesque doorway leading into the cloister from the east. In the cusps of the arch, figures holding a bishop's crozier.

37

On the left, the north wing of the transept. Rising in the centre, the famous Octagon of 1342, of which the superstructure is modern; on the right, the north side of the nave. There have been Gothic alterations to some of the windows.

38

The nave looking west to the door into the Galilee (the outside view of which is shown in Plate 33). The western transept is cut off sharply from the nave by the way in which the piers of the west crossing were strengthened in 1380. This is magnificent Romanesque architecture, strong and graceful at the same time. The arches above are nearly as large as the arches below, but divided, a screen opening into two small arches on each side of a large one, on small pillars in front of the clerestory gallery (cf. Peterborough, Plate 50). The flat painted roof has been restored. The walls are spanned with shafts which were not intended to support a vault. Only the side-aisles are vaulted.

39

In the choir, the eastern bay of the north arcade, the building of which began in 1234. Notice the unusual "half dogtooth" ornament within the richly moulded profile of the archivolts. The spandrels of the arches are filled with tracery. Beyond the arch, the Late Gothic stalagmites of Bishop Alcock's chantry chapel (1488).

40, 41, 42

The unique Octagon, built after the collapse of the Romanesque central tower in 1322, and completed in 1342. Plate 40: the view towards the nave. Plate 41: the Octagon from the north-west, on the left the nave, on the right the northern wing of the transept. Plate 42: view upwards into the lantern to the wooden star vault.

43

The Lady-chapel, a separate building reached from the north-east corner of the northern wing of the transept. It is viewed here from the east, showing the window put in in 1373. On the left, the choir.

44

The Lady-chapel, built 1320–1349. The interior, looking east to the window of 1373. An ingenious work, this chapel, of incomparable richness, an entirely independent, specifically English variation of

CANTERBURY

WINCHESTER

Gothic, which influenced the Late Gothic of France, Germany, and Spain.

45

The Lady-chapel. Detail of the blind arcade in the north wall. The points of the lower, small ogee arches cut into the more severe profile of the larger arch and terminate in pedestals for figures. Running foliage gathers thick around these pedestals. The ornamental carving and the figures are still partly gilded, the chamfering of the profile of the arch is red and light blue. The stone is white, and the shafts are of black Purbeck.

PETERBOROUGH (Northamptonshire), St. Peter's Cathedral

Plates 46–52

PETERBOROUGH has had cathedral status since 1541. The Danes in 870 destroyed the monastery-church which had been founded in the seventh century. A new church was consecrated in 952 and was burnt down in 1116, though its foundations are still there under the south wing of the transept. Abbot Jean de Séez began to build anew in 1118. The choir with three apses and no ambulatory was finished between 1140 and 1143, and the nave under Abbot Benedict between 1194 and 1197. Like Ely, Peterborough is an example of Norman-Romanesque in its full development. The centre aisle with its flat roof and the open roof above the tribune are pure Romanesque, and the side-aisles have round-arched rib vaults as at Durham. The specifically English taste for repeating the same elements again and again is very noticeable, inside and out; the use of shallow blind arcades (which are identical) in several tiers along the enormous surfaces of the wall gives an effect like tracery—a Romanesque anticipation of what is otherwise typical of Late Gothic. For a Romanesque building the interior is unusually light, partly because of the Late Gothic enlargement of the windows.

46

The choir from the south-east. The Romanesque semicircular choir of 1118–1143 was replaced by the rectangular retrochoir of 1483–1500, called the "New Building". The apses of the side-aisles were demolished (interior of the "New Building", Plate 52). The clerestory windows of the Romanesque choir were enlarged in the Late Gothic period. The central tower was restored in 1888.

47

The west front, an entirely new screen wall placed (between 1201 and 1222) in front of the old Romanesque façade. Why a master capable of anything so bold should then have made the opening in the middle much narrower instead of wider must remain a puzzle. The tower behind the gable on the left was built between 1265 and 1270. The porch in the centre is Late Gothic of 1370.

48

The south aisle of the nave, looking east. Notice the round-arched ribbed vault (cf. note to Plate 164), and the narrow arcading of round arches which intersect one another. This is a form which the Normans favoured particularly, and which they took into architecture from manuscript illumination. The windows were considerably enlarged in the Late Gothic period.

49

The north wing of the transept with the east aisle (right). A magnificent piece of Late Romanesque: the walls are almost entirely organized in plastic forms so that hardly any plain surface is left. On the outer wall there are galleries in front of both the upper rows of windows. The heroic scale of the arcades in the aisle contrasts effectively with the small blind arcades along the wall. Note that the lance-like piers are not intended to support a vault. They give a plastic accent to the wall, in association with the flat roof.

50

View from the choir through the crossing and nave to the west. On the right is the opening of the transept (Plate 49). The east and west arches of the crossing and the western arch have been altered from round to pointed. The side arcade is Romanesque. The wooden roof of the nave is fourteenth century, with old painting.

51

The head of the choir with the high altar, looking east. The pillars are alternately round and octagonal.

Above them are cushion capitals curiously simple compared with the stepped profile of the arches. The lower story of the east wall was pierced to give access to the "New Building" (cf. Plates 46 and 52). The windows of the choir are much enlarged in the Late Gothic style. The omission of the apse vault pre-scribed by tradition is unusual. Notice in the fore-ground a medieval lectern in the form of an eagle.

52

The chapel or "New Building" added behind the Romanesque choir, looking south. On the east wall (left) the Altar of Our Lady. For the exterior, see Plate 46. This chapel was built between 1483 and 1500. The fully developed fan-vault is one of the most beautiful in England. Nothing remotely com-parable exists in other European countries.

NORWICH (Norfolk), Cathedral of the Holy Trinity

Plate 7. Air Photograph (Aerofilms)

Plates 53–62

THIS is one of the purest and most imposing of the Norman abbey-cathedrals, with Late Gothic addi-tions which are easily distinguished.

In 1094 Bishop Herbert de Losinga removed the seat of the East Anglian bishopric to Norwich, and two years later he began the cathedral. At his death in 1119 the choir had been finished; the transept and the six eastern bays of the nave were finished under Eborad (1121–1145). The typically English nave is very long, with fourteen bays, three aisles, and a high tribune. The choir is similar. Typically Norman is the division of the thick walls into two in the upper stories by narrow passages. The transept is narrow and extensive, without side-aisle or triforium. Chapels open from the transept to the east. The massive central tower is open inside, its upper stories are Late Roman-esque, its stone spire is Gothic. The side-aisles are continued as an ambulatory around the semicircular choir. This anticipation of the ambulatories of the Gothic cathedrals appeared in the great pilgrim churches of the south of France in the tenth century and was general there, though uncommon in Nor-mandy and England. The circular chapels adjoining the ambulatory are unusual (the original centre chapel has been replaced by the Late Gothic Lady-chapel). Compare this arrangement with the ground-plan of Canterbury, page 19.

About 1362 the windows of the choir were renewed and their height increased (Plate 61). The choir is magnificently vaulted. Between 1446 and 1472 Bishop Lyhart replaced the flat wooden roof of the centre aisle and the transept with the rich fan-vault, in which there are 329 carved bosses. The centre porch and the great window of the west front have Late Gothic "drop tracery". The large two-storied cloister on the south side was begun in 1272.

7

Air view from the north-west. On the left of the central tower the lofty Late Gothic choir (cf. Plates 53 and 61). Left of the choir, the Lady-chapel and the northern ambulatory chapel. Beyond the nave, the cloister of 1272.

53

General view from the south-east. The central tower is Late Romanesque (middle of the twelfth century) with a Gothic steeple. The upper walls with buttresses above the Romanesque lower story of the choir were built in 1362.

54

South wing of the transept, 1096–1119. The central tower has the surface decoration characteristic of Late Romanesque in England (cf. Ely, Plates 33 and 34). The spire and the crenellation are Gothic.

55

The west front. The Romanesque portion belongs to the second half of the twelfth century. The porch and the great window are Perpendicular and were built towards the end of the fifteenth century.

56

South side of the nave (*c.* 1121–1145). The win-dows of the clerestory were enlarged in the Gothic period, the main windows are Romanesque. The cloister was begun in 1272. The tracery in the arches is Late Gothic.

57

The Prior's Door from the east bay of the south aisle into the cloister. This is in the Decorated style of the fourteenth century. It is unique.

58

The nave, looking east, with its massive simple piers. The arches of the triforium are as tall as those of the arcade. Note the clerestory with its gallery. The fine vault was built between 1446 and 1472. The choir-screen encloses four bays of the nave. The space was required for the many cathedral clergy who in England were cloistered, unlike the cathedral clergy of continental countries.

59

The west wall of the southern wing of the transept. Notice on the right the outer arch of the south aisle filled with Late Gothic tracery, and above it the tribune which extends across the wall of the transept as a gallery. This division of the thickness of the wall into two by a passage was influential in the development of Gothic.

60

The inside of the central tower, and a view into the transept. It is characteristic of England and Normandy that the central towers even of Gothic churches are kept open and well lit. The influence of this can be seen, for example, in the cathedral at Lausanne.

61

The head of the choir (surrounded by the ambulatory) and the tribune. The side arcades are Late Gothic, and the Romanesque clerestory was replaced by the much higher Gothic clerestory in 1362, with an inner passage and fan-vaulting.

62

The fan-vault of the nave, built under Bishop Lyhart (1446–1472) in place of the Romanesque timber roof. The number of ribs radiating from each pillar was increased from five to fifteen. The diagonal ribs assimilate the others, producing a net- and fan-vault in one. The ridge rib runs horizontally, the cross ribs are slightly arched (cf. Plate 58). For the ultimate form of the fan-vault with horizontal and vertical panels, see Peterborough (Plate 52) and Gloucester (Plate 109).

WINCHESTER (Hampshire), Cathedral of the Holy Trinity

Plate 4. Air photograph (Aerofilms)
Plate 10. From Britton's *Cathedral Antiquities*
Plates 63–65

WINCHESTER was the capital of the kings of Wessex in the seventh century and the bishop's seat founded here became of some importance as the place where in 827 Egbert was crowned first king of all England. Edward the Confessor was also crowned in the old minster in 1043; and William the Conqueror and some of his successors still had themselves crowned at Winchester, as their second capital, as well as in London.

The cathedral is the outcome of several complex alterations. It was originally one of the huge abbey-cathedrals which the Normans built immediately after the Conquest when they consolidated their power by appointing Norman bishops. Of the building begun by Bishop Walkelin in 1097, there remains the north wing of the transept entire (Plate 63) and the south, although this south wing is disfigured internally. The crypt with its two aisles also survives. The walls and piers of the side-aisles have a Romanesque core, but were later refaced entirely.

Behind the original ambulatory and its east chapel Robert de Lucy (1189–1202) built the immense retro-choir like a hall with three times three bays of equal height and a rectangular Lady-chapel. This eastern space substituted for the Romanesque ambulatory is also described as a "procession path". After the demolition of the ambulatory the choir and the arcades were rebuilt, and the pillars were completed about 1320. Bishop Eddington (1346–1366) began the rebuilding of the nave and the new façade, which were finished by William of Wykeham (1394–1450) and his successor. In the first quarter of the sixteenth century the

Romanesque side-aisles of the choir, which had remained till then, were rebuilt and roofed with a lierne vault. The Early Gothic Lady-chapel was rebuilt at the same time. The flat fan-vault of the crossing dates from 1635. It is, that is to say, a Gothic vault, built in the early Baroque period, which is not an uncommon occurrence in England. Winchester still has several of the most beautiful chantry chapels encased in stone tracery, and some tabernacle tombs.

4

Air view from the south-east. On the left, the long nave, which was rebuilt from the end of the fourteenth century. In the middle, the Romanesque transept of 1079; and the central tower. On the right, the choir (rebuilt in 1320 and altered again in the fifteenth century), the flat-roofed retrochoir, and the Lady-chapel projecting to the east. Retrochoir and Lady-chapel were built between 1189 and 1202, and then much altered in Late Gothic at the beginning of the sixteenth century. In the foreground, notice the monastic buildings, and the remains of the Romanesque cloister by the southern wing of the transept.

10

The northern wing of the transept (from Britton's *Cathedral Antiquities*), a magnificent and well-preserved piece of Norman-Romanesque architecture (cf. Plate 63). There is a side-aisle and triforium on each side, and a triforium resembling a tribune on the outer wall, such as one often finds in Normandy. This is the earliest example of the system by which the structural rhythm in the openings is more and more enriched up above. Notice the Norman gallery in front of the clerestory, and the timbering of the roof.

63

The west wall of the northern wing of the transept, begun in 1079 (cf. Plate 10). Note the cushion capitals merging partly into the surface of the wall.

64

The nave, looking west. This was rebuilt by Bishop Eddington (1346–1366) and by William of Wykeham (1394–1450). The core of the piers is Romanesque, and the shafts running right up them as far as the vault have not been altered except for their capitals. All the other profiles have been changed, the archivolts having been demolished and replaced by higher pointed arches at the expense of the triforium, although the arches of its openings remain behind the tracery of the window breastwork. The outer wall is practically one enormous window filled with Perpendicular tracery of the middle of the fifteenth century. On the left the fifth bay of the arcade (counting from the window) contains the chantry chapel of William of Wykeham. The pattern of the lierne vault is unusual, since the diagonal ribs do not extend straight from pillar to pillar, but cross each other before they get to the ridge. The bosses are carved with the arms, among others, of Bishop Beaufort (1405–1447) and Bishop Waynflete (1447–1486).

65

The vault of the choir, looking east. This is related to the vaulting of the nave, but it is nearer to the real fan-vault. The panels between the ribs are not convex but locked with flat slabs of stone (which is only possible when the panels are so narrow). These specifically English "panel vaults" have no counterpart abroad. The lower portions of the choir date from the rebuilding of 1320.

SALISBURY (Wiltshire), St. Mary's Cathedral

Plate 11. From Britton's *Cathedral Antiquities*

Plates 66–74

THE bishopric of Sherborne founded in the eighth century was transferred in the eleventh to Old Sarum. In the thirteenth century a cathedral was built a few miles away at New Sarum, and around this the modern city of Salisbury grew up. Salisbury Cathedral is exceptional: it is a building all of one period, completed within about forty years between 1220 and 1260. The masses are grouped on a plan which is abstract and crystalline in its clarity. The cathedral stands by itself among broad green lawns and groups of trees, surrounded some way off by small houses. The architectural detail and ornament, and particularly the design of the interior with its cramped triforium of wide arches, pressed and pressing down, may not be too convincing. Yet as a whole the cathedral is one of the most impressive buildings of Gothic architecture. James Wyatt's "pure style" restoration of 1778 to 1779 swept out many of the chantry chapels and canopy tombs.

The cathedral has an unusual screen façade (Plate 70; see also the ground-plan), and a nave of ten bays, and on the north a side door under a graceful porch with a vestibule. The great transept extends three bays in each direction with eastern side-aisles. The choir has three bays, and there is a small eastern transept of two bays in either wing, also with side-aisles on the east. Beyond stretch the three bays of the east choir or presbytery, which is aligned on the nave so that there is a view through the whole length of the seventeen bays. The view is enhanced by the fact that the walls continue as it were in the form of a peculiar bridge or buttress across the openings into the wings of the transept on either side (see Plate 73).

Behind the straight east wall of the choir is the retrochoir, with the Lady-chapel projecting to the east. The retrochoir and the Lady-chapel go up to the same height as the side-aisles, and have exquisitely graceful pillars, all angular as crystals. There is nothing rounded in the whole composition. A side door with a vestibule opens from the north aisle of the nave.

To the south is the great cloister, the interior length of each side 138 feet. The cloister opens on the east into the octagonal chapter-house of 1280 supported by a central pier of extreme slenderness (Plate 11).

Between the south aisle and the north side of the cloisters are the "plumberies", narrow spaces hidden from view which form the workshops for masons, etc., busy on the repairs required all the time in so large a structure.

11

The chapter-house on the east side of the cloister (after Britton's *Cathedral Antiquities*). Date about 1280. The slender pier has eight thin shafts and spreads into sixteen ribs. The whole space of the wall is filled with geometrical tracery of the type developed at Rheims in 1211. Notice the rich wall arcades and the carved foliage in the spandrels.

66

The southern wing of the main transept from the south-east. On the left the octagonal chapter-house (Plate 11). The other smaller octagonal building on the right (see the ground-plan), joined to the south wing of the east transept, is the vestry.

67

The north side of the cloister. Behind it and divided from it by the "plumberies" (which are invisible) rises the south wall of the nave.

68

The spire of the central tower (404 feet high) from the south. In front, almost hidden by the tree, the south wing of the main transept, and on the right the south wing of the smaller transept between the choir and the presbytery. In the foreground the monks' fishpond.

69

View from the north-east. The choir gable has groups of lancet windows which are typically English. In the front, built to the same height as the side-aisles, are the retrochoir and the projecting Lady-chapel.

70

The west façade. For another example of the frieze of quatrefoils (which form a fourth zone here and continue around the corners), see the façade at Wells (Plates 88 and 89).

71

The nave, looking west. The circular piers are surrounded by pipe-like shafts of black Purbeck marble. The simple, unfixed chairs interfere less with the feeling of space than the pews we often find on the Continent.

72

The nave. Notice how beautifully the rhythm of the arcade blends with the doubling of the side-aisle windows in each bay; but also the cramping effect of the wide triforium arches above. The canopies which belonged to many of the tombs of knights and bishops under the arches were destroyed during restoration.

73

The east bay of the choir (presbytery), and its straight east wall, with a view into the retrochoir and the Lady-chapel beyond. On the left, the curious bridging of the opening which leads into one of the wings of the narrow eastern transept. Notice also the curious form of the arches in front of the gable clerestory (which are particularly English); the variety of the arches in the arcade, and the intersection of their profile in the corners.

74

The fantastic bridge buttresses, which seem to continue the walls across the openings. These are used with even more grandeur at Wells (Plate 91). At Canterbury they are not quite so successful (Plate 17).

EXETER (Devonshire), St. Peter's Cathedral

Plate 6. Air Photograph (Aerofilms)
Plate 12. From Britton's *Cathedral Antiquities*
Plates 75–78

IN 1050 the seat of the bishop who had jurisdiction over Devon and Cornwall was moved from Crediton to Exeter. Here presumably the monastic church founded by Athelstan about 952 served as a cathedral until the Normans raised their magnificent new building.

While the French cathedrals of the thirteenth century continually surpassed each other in elegance and soared higher and higher until the vault of Beauvais reached the fantastic height of 157 feet, the English cathedrals remained more or less low and wide. Instead of height, they developed in wall and vault a richness of articulation unknown in France, though it was to influence continental architecture at the end of the fourteenth century.

Exeter is a masterpiece of weight, exuberance, dignity, and splendour. The magnificent fan-vault, with its thick ridge rib binding and uniting the liernes, harmonizes completely with the intricate moulding of the archivolts and piers, which have sixteen shafts each. Since the Romanesque aisle walls are hardly visible in the interior, Exeter Cathedral has a nearly complete unity of style.

Bishop William Warrelwast (1107–1138) began the Norman-Romanesque building in 1112. Nothing of this is left except the outer walls of the nave and, most important, the two colossal square towers which serve as transepts (they formerly had spires). The upper story of the north tower is Early Gothic.

The new building of about 1224 began with the east or Lady-chapel, a building with a single aisle, three bays and side chapels off the west bay. Adjoining this are the choir and nave following the layout of the Romanesque church. About 1270 to 1280 a rectangular chapter-house was built on to the south wing of the transept (i.e. to the south tower). In the Second World War the southern side of the choir was severely hit in one of the "Baedeker raids" by German bombers.

6

Air view from the south-west. On the right, the Lady-chapel, the oldest part of the Gothic building (1224). In the centre the two Romanesque towers, which also form a transept, and once had spires; and in front of the south tower the chapter-house.

12

The west front or façade (from Britton's *Cathedral Antiquities*). Notice the absence of towers and the

Ground-plan of Salisbury Cathedral
(from *The Builder*, 1891)

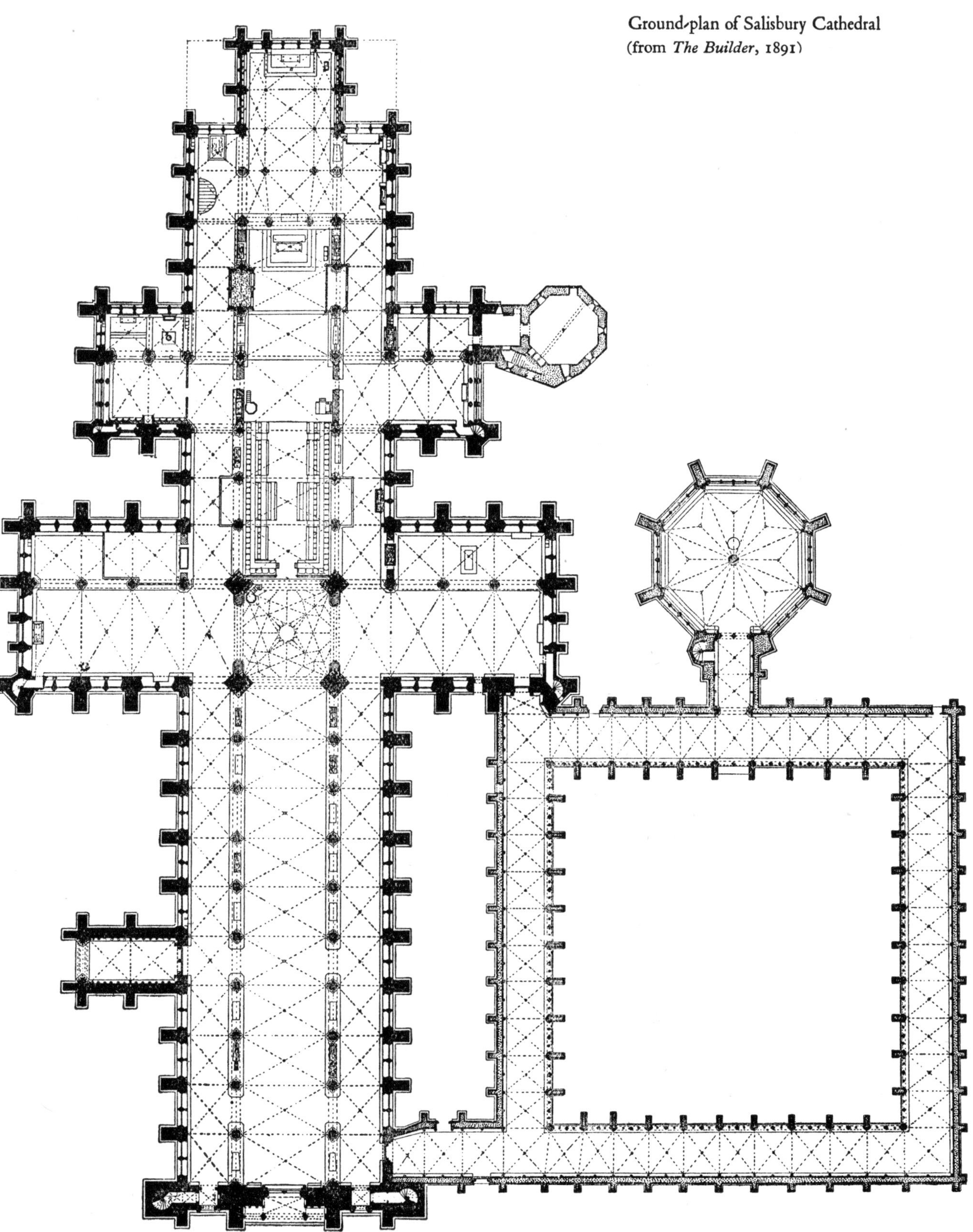

three insignificant porches in the carved screen-like construction. The great window is filled with tracery of the thirteenth century.

75

The Romanesque south tower (cf. Norwich, Plate 54). The crenellations are Late Gothic. Monastic buildings in the foreground.

76

The west façade: detail of the screen, bishops, apostles, and prophets at the side of the south (or right-hand) door.

77

The Minstrels' Gallery on the north wall of the nave (cf. Plate 78). Twelve angelic musicians are carved in relief on the front. The date is about 1340.

78

The fan-vault of the nave, looking east. Perhaps the most harmonious of all church interiors in the Decorated style, the specifically English form, that is, of High Gothic. The Minstrels' Gallery (cf. Plate 77) is on the left.

WELLS (Somersetshire), St. Andrew's Cathedral

Plate 5. Air photograph (Aerofilms)
Plates 79–100

THE bishopric of Somerset was founded at Wells in 909, and transferred in the twelfth century for a time to the fortified town of Bath. The Bishop is still known as Bishop of Bath and Wells. After Salisbury, the cathedral is the finest example of Early Gothic in England, though portions date from the High and Late Gothic periods. The general layout has been kept entire, with all the charm of a wide monastic precinct in the watered landscape from which Wells takes its name. It is one of the most perfect pictures of medievalism in all Europe.

The original building was begun by Bishop Reginald de Bohun who died in 1191. First came the three western bays of the choir (black on the plan), then the wings of the transept for the laity, followed by the crossing and the east bay of the nave. The nave was completed under Jocelyn (1206–1242) between 1220 and 1229. For England it is relatively modest, particularly in the upper stories. The rich and delicately constructed piers are very elegant, their cruciform cores surrounded by eight bundles of three shafts each, with vigorously carved capitals.

The façade (1220–1229) is unique (Plate 79; see also the plan). Behind the choir, as a retrochoir, there extends a low, hall-like space, of the most delicate construction, filled with light. From this the Lady-chapel, slightly higher, juts out to the east. It was completed by Master William Joyce in 1326, and the retrochoir was built between 1320 and 1363. The three east bays of the choir (i.e. the presbytery) and the upper stories of its western bays were rebuilt at the same time.

The two-storied octagonal chapter-house is entered from the western bay of the north aisle of the choir. The lower story resembles a crypt, the upper is shown in Plate 100.

5

Air view from the east. Right in front is the Lady-chapel, and behind it the low retrochoir, on the right the octagonal two-storied chapter-house, and the gate-house, or "Chain Gate", leading to the double row of small houses known as the "Vicar's Close" (see Plates 83, 84, 99). On the left of the cathedral the enormous cloister (which measures inside about 180 by 120 feet). Next to this comes the Bishop's palace in its fine park, on the extreme left.

79

The west façade, 1220–1239. The upper story of the unfinished south tower dates from 1367 to 1386, and of the north tower from 1407 to 1424. The screen rising from the green expanse of turf is fantastic and unique; the towers stand at the sides of the nave, and not over the western bays of the side-aisles, which is the usual plan on the Continent. The porch is insignificant; the disproportionately high plinth on either side actually forms the jamb! The upper zone contains the richest and most beautiful figure cycle of English

SALISBURY

EXETER 12

YORK 13

Ground-plan of Wells Cathedral
(from *The Builder*, 1891)

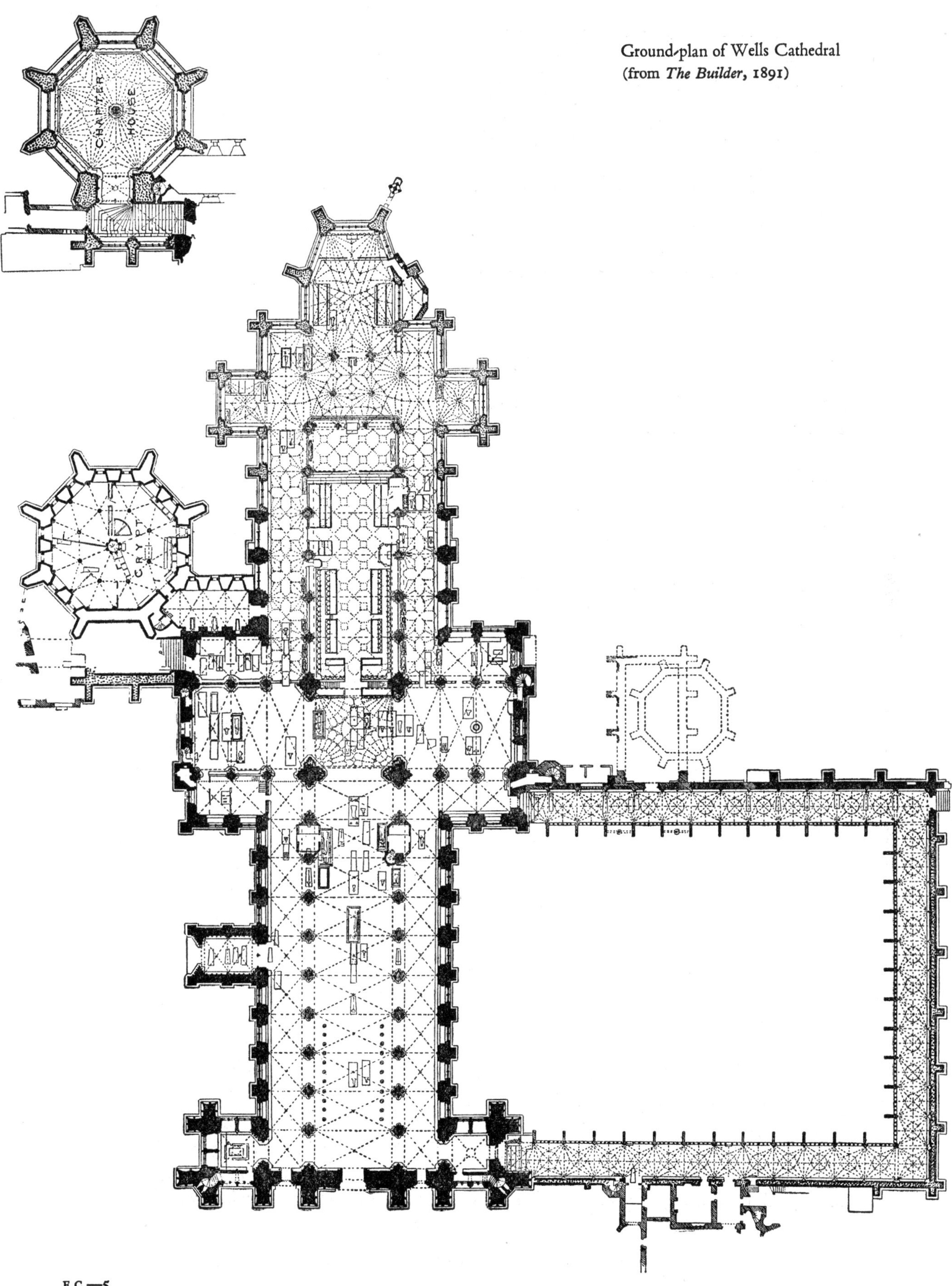

Gothic, consisting of 350 figures. On the left, the gatehouse with a passage above it leading from the chapter-house to the "Vicar's Close" (cf. Plate 84).

80

From the south-west. In the foreground the market-place with the gate known as "Brown's Gate", or the "Dean's Eye", and the "Penniless Porch", built by Bishop Beckington (1443–1465).

81

View from the south-east. In front, hidden by the poplars, the Lady-chapel; on the right of it the chapter-house, built (an unusual arrangement) in two stories.

82

South side of the cathedral. In the foreground the moat of the Bishop's palace.

83

The "Vicar's Close", containing the double row of forty-two small houses built in the fourteenth century by Richard of Shrewsbury as dwellings for the cathedral choristers, and altered in the fifteenth century. At the far end of the two rows, looking south, the gatehouse, the chapter-house, and the cathedral. To the north, the road between the houses terminates in a chapel (cf. also Plate 5).

84

The "Chain Gate", or gatehouse erected by Bishop Beckington, carrying a passage between the cathedral and the "Vicar's Close". At the back the chapter-house, in front the staircase (Plate 99) and the north wing of the transept.

85

The north tower from the north-east. The two lower stories were built between 1220 and 1229, the upper story dates from 1407 to 1427. The two intersecting arches in the middle story are one of the earliest examples of the Gothic interpenetration of profiles (cf. also Plate 89). Left of the tower, the north porch of about 1240, which has a beautiful interior.

86–89

Details from the west façade (for other examples of quatrefoils carried on round a corner of the buttresses, see Plate 69).

90

View from the centre aisle to the north-east. Heavy but elegantly constructed piers with twenty-four shafts. The boldly curving, more or less abstract foliage of the capitals anticipates as early as the middle of the thirteenth century the formal ideas of Late Gothic. The monotonous tribune and the plain windows are rather meagre.

91

The nave, looking east to the highly fantastic buttress arch of the crossing, added in 1338 (cf. Plate 94). For a similar effect, but less extreme, at Salisbury, see Plates 73 and 74.

92

A capital from one of the piers in the nave—an ingenious variation of the Early Gothic crocket capital. The carved scene is the grape harvest. It is not the whole of the pillar which has a capital, but the individual shafts attached to it. This is an anticipation of Late Gothic.

93

A capital in the retrochoir, 1360—a leaf cluster of thickly interlaced Late Gothic foliation, developed from naturalistic oak leaves and acorns. The clustered capitals commonly found in the fifteenth century are interlaced even more thickly.

94

The crossing with the buttress arch of 1338 (cf. Plate 91). Such a thing would have been inconceivable abroad.

95

East part of the choir (the presbytery) with a view into the retrochoir and Lady-chapel. The choir has a straight east wall and the retrochoir replaces the usual polygonal ambulatory of the Continent. The portions shown in the photograph were rebuilt about 1320–1363; from the third bay onwards (right foreground) only the upper stories have been restored. A unique building of extraordinary richness. All the wall surfaces are covered with stone tracery, which is employed as a rule only around the altar or for single tombs. Note the passage in front of the clerestory, and the fantastic net-vaulting. On the right by the fourth pillar is the pinnacled tomb canopy of Bishop Beckington (died 1465), behind it the enclosed chantry chapel of Bishop Harwell.

96

The retrochoir, south wing. On the left, view into the Lady-chapel. The window on the left has geometrical tracery (1325), the window on the right, flowing tracery (1360), which reached France about 1370 and appeared all over the Continent as Flamboyant. In England it soon gave way to Perpendicular, or Recti-linear, tracery (e.g. Plate 106). Notice between the windows the tomb canopy with tall pinnacles, dating from the end of the thirteenth century.

97

The southern side of the cloister built in the second half of the fourteenth century. Notice the beautiful harmony of the structure of vault and wall.

98

A small corbel figure on the east wall of the chapter-house staircase: a monk with a stick killing one of the vices in the form of a dragon.

99

Staircase branching off from the east of the northern wing of the transept. Straight ahead is the porch leading into the "Vicar's Close" above the "Chain Gate" (Plate 84), on the right the entrance to the upper chapter-house (Plate 100).

100

The chapter-house: the main floor of the two-storied octagonal building, finished about 1319. The core of the central pier is surrounded by sixteen slender shafts of black Purbeck marble, and above it is the fan of thirty-two ribs. Eleven ribs radiate from each angle of the polygon. The small space is thus vaulted by forty-four cross ribs, eight radial ribs, and a ridge rib following the form of the octagon.

GLOUCESTER (Gloucestershire), Cathedral of the Holy Trinity

Plate 3. Air photograph (Aerofilms)

Plates 101–110

THE abbey of Gloucester was founded in the seventh century as a nunnery and later sheltered a school for lay-priests. In 1022 the Benedictines arrived. An earlier church was burnt down, and under the Benedictines work started in 1089 upon the Norman-Romanesque building of the great abbey-church of St. Peter. In 1540, after the Reformation, the abbey-church became a cathedral and was re-dedicated to the Holy Trinity. It is one of the most important and problematic buildings in the history of art. Here, if anywhere, an entirely new conception of form appears at one stroke—the conception of English Late Gothic. It was to last for centuries, and played a decisive part in the Gothic Revival.

Of the Romanesque work much remains. In the nave (unusual in having no tribune) there are massive circular pillars 31 feet high and 6½ feet in diameter. The choir, to the east of the simple transept, does have a tribune which also follows the ambulatory with its three radiating chapels. Following the same ground-plan, there is also an extensive crypt. In 1240 the old wooden roof of the central aisle of the nave was re-placed with a ribbed vault, which joins the wall low down and cuts off the top of the Romanesque win-dows. The Romanesque crypt, the ambulatory with the tribune, and the walls of the southern wing of the transept remain unchanged, but the interior of the choir has been altogether transformed.

The south aisle was rebuilt between 1318 and 1329, and the southern wing of the transept alongside was remodelled between 1331 and 1337. In this work the flattened "keel" arch, a form of four-centred arch, appeared for the first time. The buttress of the crossing pier and the tracery of the wall are assimilated with extraordinary boldness (Plate 103). The choir and the northern wing of the transept were altered between 1337 and 1377. The piers in the choir are split in two vertically, and a thin trellis of stone has been raised in front of the Romanesque arcade and triforium. Thus wall surfaces and openings alike are veiled by a net-work of stone. The rounded end of the choir itself has been broken off to give place to an opening in the east wall in the shape of a lattice of stone and stained glass (Plate 106). Behind, and almost separate, comes the Lady-chapel, finished between 1472 and 1499. The two western bays and the west façade with its great window were built by Abbot Morewent (1421–1437), as well as the side door in the south wing of the tran-sept. The central tower is unusually magnificent and graceful, in spite of its massiveness. It was begun by

Abbot Seabroke (1450–1457). The height is 225 feet. The fittings are rich, with interesting tombs. The magnificent cloister has an unusual position on the north side of the church. The east wing, which has the earliest fan-vault in the pure style, dates from 1351 to 1377, the other wings of the cloister date from 1381 to 1412.

3

Air view from the south-east. On the right, the choir and Lady-chapel. Notice the cloister curiously placed on the north of the church (Plates 101–110).

101

From the north: the central tower, 225 feet high (typical of Somerset and Gloucestershire), below it the Romanesque northern wing of the transept ending in a Gothic window of about 1377.

102

The arcade of the nave, looking through into the north aisle. Contrary to French usage, there is no ornamental correspondence between arch and pillar, and instead of a tribune there is a mere passage. The Early Gothic vault of 1240 unfortunately cuts into the windows, which are placed unusually high; the tracery in these Romanesque windows is Late Gothic, *c.* 1410. The zigzag pattern carved out of the body of the arches is unusual.

103

East wall of the south aisle, a Romanesque wall faced with Gothic masonry of 1331–1337. In almost every detail the Gothic forms are novel, a fantastic mixture of genius and whimsicality. The staircase on the left leads into the ambulatory raised above the crypt. Next to it, on the right, a staircase leads down into the crypt itself. On the far right, below the buttress, can be seen the chapel at the east of the transept (the motive of a buttress carried through the wall is repeated in the nave at Worcester, Plate 116).

104

Entrance to the northern wing of the transept which was remodelled in the Gothic style between 1337 and 1377. Notice the inventiveness shown in the solution of the vaulting. The pendent fans are hardly thinkable without Islamic influence; but if there was such influence it has been translated entirely into Gothic idiom and masonry. The thin distended keel arches are a form of the four-centred arch. Notice the net-vaulting in the transept.

105

The lierne vault of the presbytery. The diagonal ribs run between alternate pillars. The bosses are carved with figures and foliage. Such a vault has not even the remotest parallel abroad.

106

The east wall of the choir, 72 feet high and 38 feet wide. This was erected between 1347 and 1350 in place of the Romanesque east wall, but the Romanesque side-aisles survive behind the Gothic facing. Here you see the essence of Late Gothic, or Perpendicular, tracery. The arcades on either side are filled in with tombs.

107

The Lady-chapel to the east of the choir, looking west; completed between 1472 and 1499 under Abbot Farley. It is a single-aisled, lantern-like space without any plain wall-surface, and it must be considered a masterpiece of that Perpendicular style first developed here at Gloucester in the choir. Over the entrance into the choir is the tribune, reached from the tribune of the ambulatory by the "Whispering Gallery" (so called because of its acoustics).

108

The lierne vault of the Lady-chapel, with, as it were, three ridge ribs. Basically this is a pointed barrel-vault to which the net of ribs is attached as an ornament without structural significance.

109

The south wing of the cloister. Notice on the left, under every arch, the two niches where the monks sat and wrote (the scriptorium). One of the chief occupations of the medieval monk was copying manuscripts on parchment and illuminating them with initials, miniatures, and ornaments. On the north side of the cloister is the monks' "lavatorium", on the east the earliest fully developed fan-vault of any size (1351–1377). The other wings are also vaulted. Vaulting of this kind became general in England and lasted into the seventeenth century.

110

The south side of the cloister, with a door leading into the north aisle. Notice the honeycomb tracery.

HEREFORD (Herefordshire),
Cathedral of St. Mary and St. Ethelbert

Plates 111–114

St. Ethelbert was murdered in 794 and miracles took place at his tomb in Hereford, which became the seat of an Anglo-Saxon bishopric. As it stands, the cathedral is a medley of Late Romanesque and Gothic elements, much restored. Portions have not merely been altered, but some of them entirely renewed. Of the original building begun by the first Norman bishop, Robert de Losinga (1079–1095), there are only fragments left, dating from the middle of the twelfth century. The nave up to the level of the arcade is Romanesque. The massive stepped arches are patterned with zigzag above round squat pillars. The upper stories were entirely rebuilt by James Wyatt after the collapse of the western towers in 1786 and the nave was then shortened by one bay. The new façade was built between 1902 and 1908. The south wing of the transept is also Romanesque, but Gothicized in 1400, as were the arcade and the triforium levels of the choir. The clerestory above them is Early English. At the east end, additions were made in the fourteenth century which have the effect of a transept. The Lady-chapel (which is not architecturally distinguished) projects from these transept-like additions to the east.

Far the most interesting point of Hereford is the northern wing of the transept, Early Decorated of about 1260, whimsical and decidedly English in form (Plate 114). Of the fourteenth-century cloister only two and a half sides survive. In the west wing of the cloister is the famous library with its chained folios. There are several tombs.

111

View from the south-west. The central tower belongs to the second half of the fourteenth century. It has lost the spire it still had in the eighteenth century. In the foreground, the medieval bridge over the Wye.

112

The central tower. On the left, the choir and below it the northern wing of the transept-like additions to the east. On the right, the northern wing of the transept with unusually shaped windows.

113

The nave. On the Late Romanesque pillars notice the disproportionately thin shafts which probably were connected with a flat roof. The triforium and the clerestory were built by James Wyatt in the eighteenth century. The alabaster effigy on the tomb is that of Sir Richard Pembridge.

114

The east side of the northern arm of the transept. Notice how the ornamented arches of the arcade and triforium bend sharply just above the springing, and then rise almost without a curve, like beams. This is an isolated anticipation in 1260 or thereabouts of the Late Gothic four-centred arch. The spandrels of the triforium arcade are filled with diaper work. The clerestory windows are composed of circles with six divisions, three such circles forming a triangle within a lancet-shaped niche. The corbels of the piers of the vault are unusual in shape, like cornets. The smallest shafts in the composite pillars are made of black Purbeck marble. The tomb is that of Bishop Thomas de Cantilupe, who died in 1283.

WORCESTER (Worcestershire), Cathedral of Christ and Our Lady

Plates 115–123

ORIGINALLY the foundation at Worcester was one for lay-priests. In the tenth century Bishop Oswald transformed it into a Benedictine monastery and refounded the church of St. Peter. The cathedral was destroyed by the Danes, and Bishop Wulfstan (1062–1095) undertook a new building on the same site. In 1202 miracles at Wulfstan's grave (he was canonized in 1203) began to attract pilgrims.

Of the building St. Wulfstan began in 1084, there survive the four-aisled crypt and the core of the crossing piers and parts of the aisle walls, as well as the wings of the west transept. The façade and the two bays of the nave next to it are Late Romanesque with Gothic additions of the last quarter of the fourteenth century. The round chapter-house with a massive vault and a heavy circular pillar in the centre dates from the second half of the twelfth century. The polygonal facing of the chapter-house is Gothic.

The new Gothic building began with the east choir or presbytery, consecrated with much pomp in 1218. The centre aisle projects one bay to the east to form a Lady-chapel (which was entirely renovated in 1855). The tribune-like triforium has a remarkable unity. The archivolts are marked by an indescribable diversity and fineness of moulding. The triforium is closed by a blind arcaded wall at the back and not left open to the rafters as it is at Lincoln. The graceful arcaded screen in front of the clerestory is all part of the harmony and unity of design. Black Purbeck marble has been used lavishly on shafts, columns, imposts, and cornices. In fact the interior is one of the noblest monuments of the Early English style. The narrow eastern transept and the west choir (of which the foundation stone was laid in 1224) are similar in form with slightly wider arcades. The Romanesque nave was demolished except for the west bay. The north side was rebuilt *c.* 1317–1327, when work was interrupted by the plague. The centre aisle was vaulted in 1377. The western transept was rebuilt in Perpendicular style in 1336 and the central tower erected between 1358 and 1374 when the Romanesque west end was given a Gothic facing. The great west window was renewed in the nineteenth century. The cathedral is especially rich in monuments and burial chapels of every kind. There is a cloister, built after 1374, and monastic buildings.

115

The central tower (1358–1374) from the north-west, beyond the Severn.

116

The nave, looking east. The north side was built 1317–1327, and the vault in 1377. The Late Romanesque west bay is not visible. In the bay before the crossing, notice the buttress arch projecting at an angle from the wall surface, as at Gloucester (Plate 103). The nave is beautifully contrasted from the older choir, because of the different form of the pillars, the crocket capitals, and the use of Purbeck marble.

117

The south aisle of the nave, looking west. On the left, the Romanesque wall. The unusual vault dates from the end of the fourteenth century.

118

The north-east corner of the smaller eastern transept. Right, the east choir, built in 1218. Shafts and mouldings of polished Purbeck. Notice the beauty of the crocket capitals.

119

The north wing of the cloister, begun in 1374. A net-vault of magnificent form with panel-vaults between the ribs (cf. Plate 65), and richly carved bosses. In the east wing there are niches in the wall for books, in the west wing provisions for washing.

120–123

Details from the vault of the cloister. Plates 120 and 121, the Coronation of the Virgin, surrounded by angels and kings. Plate 122, the Madonna enthroned with angels. Plate 123, the Tree of Jesse, from which the ancestors of Christ branch off along the ridge rib. Above, King David with his harp as the forefather of Christ.

LICHFIELD (Staffordshire), Cathedral of St. Mary and St. Chad

Plate 8. Air photograph (Aerofilms)
Plates 124–128

THE seat of the bishops of Mercia was transferred from Repton to Lichfield by St. Chad. In 700 Bishop Hedda erected the first church on the site of the present cathedral, but nothing is left of it nor of the twelfth-century Norman cathedral. The whole cathedral is Gothic. The three west bays of the choir and the southern wing of the transept date from about 1220, the northern wing of the transept from about 1240, the nave after 1250 and the façade from 1280. The eastern bay of the choir (the presbytery) and the Lady-chapel added to the eastward, and the upper stories and vault of the choir and transept were all built between the end of the thirteenth century and the middle of the fourteenth. The building is entirely of red sandstone, much renewed, especially on the façade, first after the ravages of the seventeenth century and then from 1877.

8

Air view from the north-west. On the left, the rather low Lady-chapel extending from the choir. In the angle between the choir and the northern wing of the transept the octagonal oblong of the chapter-house built about 1250 (cf. Plate 128).

124

The west façade, begun about 1280. All the figures (and the spires) were renewed in the nineteenth century. Compared with French cathedrals built at the same time, the compactness of the towers, their confused connexion with the lower story, and the mean articulation of the building seem old-fashioned. The monotonous sequence of blind tracery on the plain wall surfaces is specifically English, not to mention the insignificance of the porches, which are the main motif of every French façade.

125

The Lady-chapel at the east end of the choir, built in the first half of the fourteenth century. The parapet (already found in the façade of St. Denis about 1440, and then at Rheims) is an architectural reference to the "fortress of Zion". Left, vaulted burial niches between the buttresses, each canopy with a pointed arch.

126

View from the south into the north wing of the transept, built about 1240. The vault has the typically English ridge rib with the added diagonals. It is an early form of fan-vault, dating from the end of the thirteenth to the beginning of the fourteenth century.

127

The nave looking towards the east where the view is closed by the Lady-chapel. The altar and choir screen are new. The nave was built in the second half of the thirteenth century, and the pillars were strengthened by enormously tall, thin, filleted shafts. The profiles are diffused. The unusual circular tracery in the spandrels of the arcade is cut by the vault shafts (as at Séez, in Normandy). In spite of appearances, there is no real tribune in the second story but merely a dark space above the roof of the aisle below. The clerestory windows are arrangements of triple circles. The vault resembles that in the transept (Plate 126). All the profiles in the upper stories are carved with dogtooth ornament, as though glittering with diamonds.

128

The chapter-house, about 1250. An octagonal oblong in shape. The central pillar is surrounded by ten shafts, and supports a fan of sixteen ribs.

LINCOLN (Lincolnshire), St. Mary's Cathedral

Plates 129–148

In 1072 Remigius (Rémy de Fécamp) removed his see from Dorchester-on-Thames to Lincoln and at once began to build a cathedral worthy of the commanding position he had chosen for it. It is a huge complex building, mainly (though parts of the façade are Romanesque) Early and High Gothic, with later additions. Moreover it is full of experiments in construction of every kind, in vaulting, and in ornament. The black Purbeck marble has been used for capitals and shafts, in foliation and in blind arcading along the walls, with an inexhaustible diversity. No continental church comes near Lincoln in magnificence and richness of detail. Work on the Norman building, begun by Remigius, went on until the middle of the twelfth century. It is to this period that the Late Romanesque portions of the façade belong (Plate 131. In the plan the Romanesque parts of the façade are marked in black). What the builders originally intended it is difficult to determine; and it is curious that the grand theme of the niches in the façade was not used again so as to contrive a really impressive portal.

The Gothic building began with the eastern transept, in 1192. The builder was Master Geoffrey de Noyers under Bishop Hugo of Avalon (1186–1200). It still shows some older characteristics: thus the chapels on the east side are semicircular. Next came the forechoir of three bays and the great western transept which has side-aisles along the east of each wing, each containing three chapels—by this time, however, with straight east walls in contrast with the semicircular chapels of the earlier transept. The collapse of the tower made it necessary to strengthen the piers of the crossing in 1239. After this the façade was completed in the Gothic style, together with the space adjoining it on the east. The nave with its seven bays was vaulted in 1233 and shows the first attempt to enrich the ribs. No such development appears abroad.

East of the smaller transept are the presbytery and the retrochoir, built between 1256 and 1320. Known as "the Angel Choir", from the figures which adorn it (Plates 146, 147), the retrochoir is a brilliant early example of the Decorated English High Gothic style. This style does develop like the continental *style rayonnant* as it appears round about 1230 in the new building of St. Denis and the Sainte Chapelle in Paris. However, it multiplies ornament to an extraordinary degree and moves without transition from Early to Late Gothic. Lincoln has exceptionally rich porches with vestibules, especially the one of 1230 on the west side of the southern wing of the transept. On the north side of the choir the chapel called Fleming's Chantry was added in 1494, and on the south side Russel's Chantry and Longland's Chantry with the choir porch between them (Plate 135). As at Gloucester, the decagonal chapter-house and the cloister are placed on the north side, contrary to the usual custom.

129

The cathedral on its height, magnificently commanding the whole city. The west towers, partly concealed by the façade, are Romanesque below. John of Welbourne (who died in 1380) carried them higher, and their spires were demolished in 1807. This view looks eastward from the castle. In front of the cathedral is the Exchequer Gate.

130

From the south-west. The central tower on the right was rebuilt after collapsing in 1239. The upper stories date from 1307 to 1311. English cathedral convents were generally set apart within their own precincts, but like continental cathedrals, Lincoln is right in the city.

131

The west façade. The Romanesque portions of 1150, the Gothic *c.* 1220–1230. Above the centre porch the Gothic frieze with the figures of kings (Plate 132). The Romanesque frieze can be seen on the extreme right (Plate 133). The surface of the gable is patterned with trellis work (gauffrure) which was perhaps suggested by Islamic wall-facings of patterned brick or tiles, like the later diaper pattern (Plate 142).

132

Gothic figures of the fourteenth century added later above the Romanesque central porch (Plate 131).

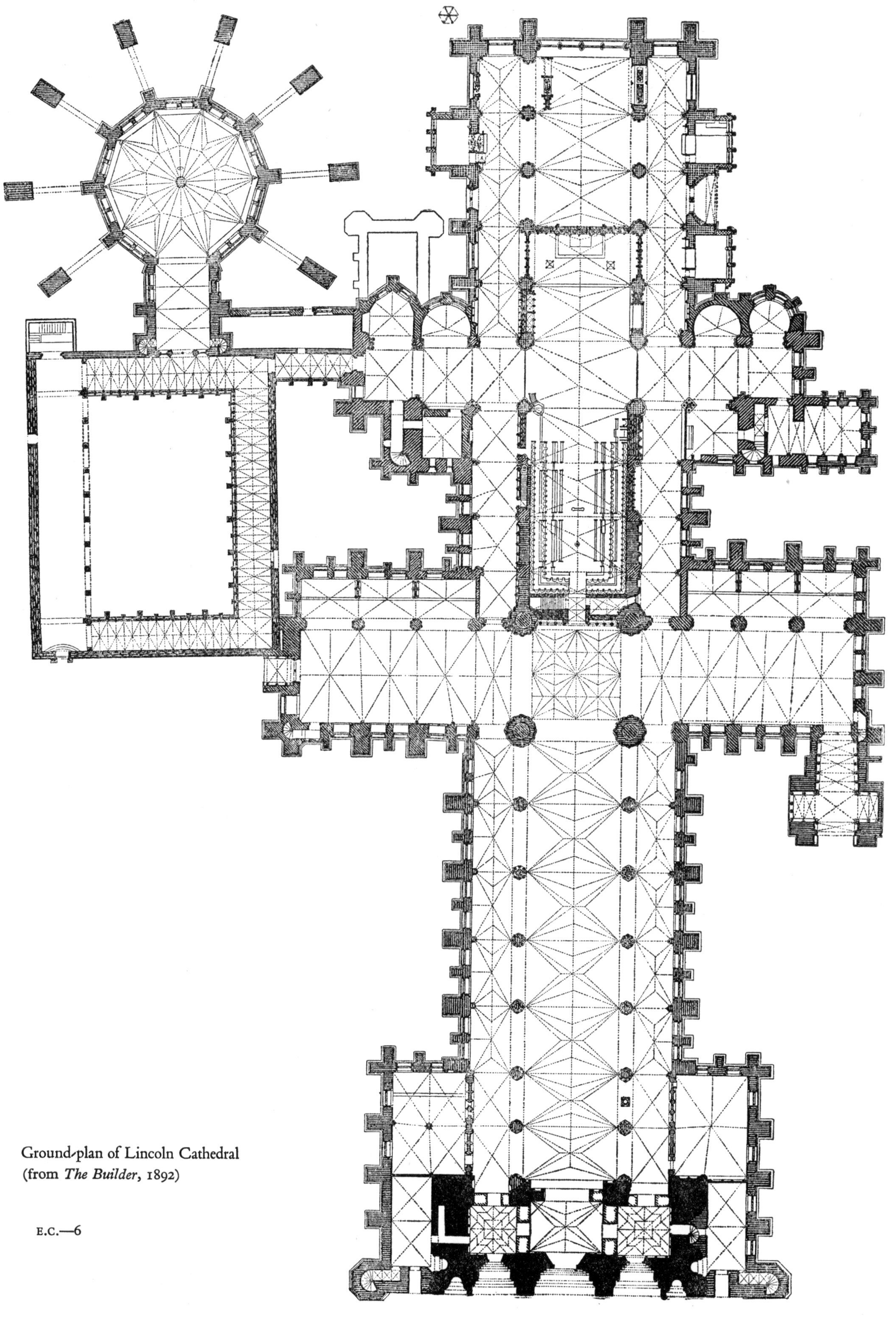

Ground-plan of Lincoln Cathedral
(from *The Builder*, 1892)

E.C.—6

133

Romanesque relief above the smaller porch to the right, of about 1150 (Plate 131). On the left, Noah building the ark in the form of a Norse dragon ship. Within the frame, Daniel in the lion's den. On the right, the ark coming to land, and God talking with Noah.

134

Carved Norman shafts, the heads of demons and the zigzag ornaments of the west porch. The fantastic foliage clutching the left-hand shaft with tendrils like an octopus resemble the illuminations in eleventh-century manuscripts of the Winchester School. Up the other shaft, tendrils, naked figures, and fabulous beasts, which are probably derived from late antique models transmitted either through illuminated MSS. or through ivory carvings. On the right, the heads of the demons bind the shaft to the wall with their beards and tongues. The ornamented cushion capitals date from about the middle of the twelfth century.

135

The south porch of the Angel Choir (1270), flanked by two Late Gothic chantry chapels. On the right, Russel's Chantry (1494). On the left, Longland's Chantry (*c.* 1521–1530). In the tympanum of the porch, a relief of the Last Judgement. Notice in the pointed gable typical Norman tracery as though cut out with the aid of a template. Similar examples may be seen in Bayeux, Coutance, and elsewhere in Normandy.

136

The statue of Queen Margaret on the outside of the Angel Choir, at the right-hand corner of Russel's Chantry.

137

The east gable of the Angel Choir, with geometrical tracery. For the interior see Plates 143 and 144.

138

The chapter-house of 1220, from the east. A decagon, with free-standing buttresses. Inside it has a central pillar and a star vault of twenty radiating ribs. On the left, the northern wing of the east transept.

139

The nave and the north aisle. As at Salisbury (Plate 72) there are two aisle windows to each bay, but the vault is more richly designed. A particular charm of Lincoln is the variety of the blind wall arcades below the windows of the aisle. Here they take the form of gently curved trefoil arches above small composite pillars of Purbeck marble with smooth rounded capitals. In the choir there are two screens of similar arcades crossing one another. Others have rich foliate capitals, and so on. Notice above the arcade the cross between a tribune and a mere triforium, with a space (though a very dark one) behind the arcade. These arches are more in harmony with the arcade below than the ones at Salisbury. The spandrels are pierced by uniform geometrical figures rather than tracery, the three clerestory windows have a gallery and are screened with five narrow arches. The vault in form and tempo harmonizes with the profiles of arch and pillar. It was completed in 1223. Notice the way in which some of the ribs disappear into the wall without reaching the small capital of the vaulting shaft, which is supported on a corbel. This is an early example of such cutting away, which is otherwise more typical of Late Gothic. The pier in the foreground is surrounded by separate black shafts of polished Purbeck marble. The crocket capital is of light-coloured stone, the abacus again of dark.

140

The centre aisle, looking east. The clear ridge rib appears to bind and unite the whole vault. The wall space surrounding the arches of the crossing is covered with diaper work. Below the organ stretches the stone choir-screen (Plate 142).

141

The springing of the arch in the porch of the southern wing of the transept in the lower choir (at Lincoln the side-aisles are also cut off by the choir-screen). Here you see the highest development of the Early Gothic idiom, which appears only in England. On the Continent at this time (mid-thirteenth century) this development is replaced by the *style rayonnant*. Purbeck shafts divide the mouldings of dogtooth and rosette. The thickly foliated capitals are already developing towards Late Gothic.

142

The stone choir-screen (*c.* 1300–1320). Formerly coloured, this is magnificent work in the Decorated style, every scrap of surface covered with rosette-patterned diaper. The diaper was probably derived from Islamic tiles, but it was infinitely more laborious to cut such patterns out of stone. There are similar designs in the damascene backgrounds of French and English illuminated MSS. during this period. Here and in the related screen at Southwell the Late Gothic idiom is emerging from the scarcely developed High Gothic of the Parisian masters of the mid-thirteenth century.

143

The Angel Choir, looking eastward. Here (as at Ely), the ambulatory (or "procession path"), the retrochoir and the Lady-chapel are in fact a single spatial unit divided ritually not architecturally. The date is between 1256 and 1320. In the Angel Choir the Early Gothic style is raised to the highest pitch of magnificence in the east window and in the triforium arches above the arcade, as well as in the blind wall arcading formed from the geometrical tracery of the High Gothic (*style rayonnant*). In the spandrels of the triforium arches the angelic musicians play their instruments. Everywhere an abundance of graceful foliage surrounds the windows, the tribune arches and the corbels of the delicate shafts of the vault. Carving glimmers in the archivolts; and everything (although of a fantastic splendour by continental standards) has a certain happy freshness. All the same, the single elements have not yet quite coalesced here into the new style as they have in the choir-screen (Plate 142). In the foreground, the high altar and the presbytery.

144

The east end of the Angel Choir, behind the high altar. Some of the glass in the windows is thirteenth century. In front of the east window are remains of the tomb of Queen Eleanor of Castile, who died in 1290.

145

The tribune-like triforium of the Angel Choir. In France, after the building of Chartres, which began in 1194, it became the rule to compose the triforium much more strictly as a binding arcade which was narrow and horizontal. England continued to use the Early Gothic tribune, often, as here, in an indecisive transition. Note the exuberant employment of Purbeck marble.

146

Angelic musicians on the south wall of the Angel Choir.

147

A spandrel in the triforium of the Angel Choir. Madonna and Child and an angel swinging a censer. The extreme elongation of the figure of the Child is typically English.

148

Portion of a blind arch in the northern side-aisle of the choir. The boldly carved foliage grows like a plant, is fleshy, and yet by no means naturalistic (cf. Plate 146). In the groove between the shafts, a row of dogtooth.

YORK (Yorkshire), York Minster, St. Peter's Cathedral

Plate 2. Air photograph (Aerofilms)

Plate 13. From Britton's *Cathedral Antiquities*

Plates 149–157

YORK Minster stands where Paulinus, the first Bishop of York, baptized Edwin, King of Northumbria, on the Easter Sunday of 627. Since the eleventh century the archbishop has borne the title of a primate of England, and in the Church of England he ranks immediately after the Archbishop of Canterbury.

In 1080 Thomas of Bayeux, the first Norman bishop, began to rebuild the cathedral. The ground-plan today is larger than that of any other medieval church in England. Inside, in the height and slenderness of its arcades, York comes nearer the French cathedrals than any of the others illustrated in this book.

Most of the crypt survives from the Romanesque building, and it contains also fragments of an early medieval fabric of the eighth century. Otherwise it is a Gothic structure on Romanesque foundations. The piers of the crossing (black on the plan) have possibly, though, a Romanesque core. The three-aisled nave has eight bays, the transept also has three aisles, and the massive central tower has an open in- terior. Since a metropolitan church had so many clergy, the choir is larger than the nave by one bay. The actual choir is made up of the four western bays, containing the choir stalls. The fifth bay forms an eastern transept, discernible in the layout only by the greater richness of its vaulting; this was achieved by raising the aisle bays to the same height as the central aisle. The three eastern bays form a retrochoir with an altar to Our Lady against the straight east wall. Nearly all the windows are rich with remains of old stained glass.

The rebuilding of the Minster in the Gothic styles began between 1230 and about 1241 with the southern wing of the transept (Plate 150). The northern wing was rebuilt between 1341 and 1360. In this wing are the "Five Sisters", five high, narrow lancet-windows, filled with old stained glass, on the outer wall (Plate 13). The nave was built between 1291 and 1324. The triforium, with five arches to each bay, is treated as a socle for the clerestory windows. The aisle walls have rich canopied arcades. Above the main aisle the wooden vault was renewed in 1890. The presbytery was built between 1361 and 1370 with windows of an interesting form. In the eastern half of the choir the clerestory is glazed on the inner side of the gallery which divides the wall in two, while outside there is an unglazed screen of stone tracery. In the western half of the choir, this arrangement is reversed, passage inside, windows outside.

2

Air view from the south-east. On the left is the nave of 1291 to 1324 with the west towers of 1433 to 1470, the southern wing of the transept (cf. Plate 150), then the choir, east transept, and presbytery. The octagonal chapter-house is behind.

13

The octagonal chapter-house, from Britton's *Cathedral Antiquities*. It was completed in 1342 with a wooden star vault lacking any support in the centre. On the right of the chapter-house, the northern wing of the transept (1241–1260), showing the Five Sisters. The central tower above (1400–1423), and the nave adjoining it to the right.

149

The west façade. By English standards the porch is notable. Up to the roof of the nave the façade was completed in 1338. The south tower was built between 1433 and 1477, the north tower between 1470 and 1474, and the central tower between 1400 and 1423.

150

The gable of the southern wing of the transept (1230–1241), and the south-west tower. The two gables of the transept are among the most beautiful examples of the Early English style (also called "lanceolate" because of the lancet shape of the win- dows, which contain no tracery) in its full flower. Dogtooth ornament runs round the windows (cf. Plate 114). The rose-window is awkwardly com- pressed into the top of the gable. In the French proto- type it would have been placed lower down as the main window.

151

The nave (1291–1321), and beyond it the crossing and the choir. Notice that the arcades are tall and narrow, with the piers powerfully constructed, and the aisle windows large. On the Continent these windows are mostly replaced by side chapels added later between buttresses. Coats of arms are added in the spandrels of the arches. The wooden vault was renewed in 1890. For the choir-screen see Plate 157.

152–155

Capitals in the nave (152, 153, 154) and in the crossing (155). These show how the simple cushion capital becomes the carved capital in which the foliage does not spring out of the shafts, but winds round the pillar like a separate wreath. Plate 153: a foliate capital, Late Gothic. In Plates 153 and 155 the abacus is reduced to a narrow cornice.

156

The inside of the central tower (1400–1423). In France the greater height at the crossing was aban- doned in favour of a more restful and harmonious spatial effect. In England and in Normandy this magnificent though fundamentally Romanesque theme of the open tower was retained into the Late Gothic.

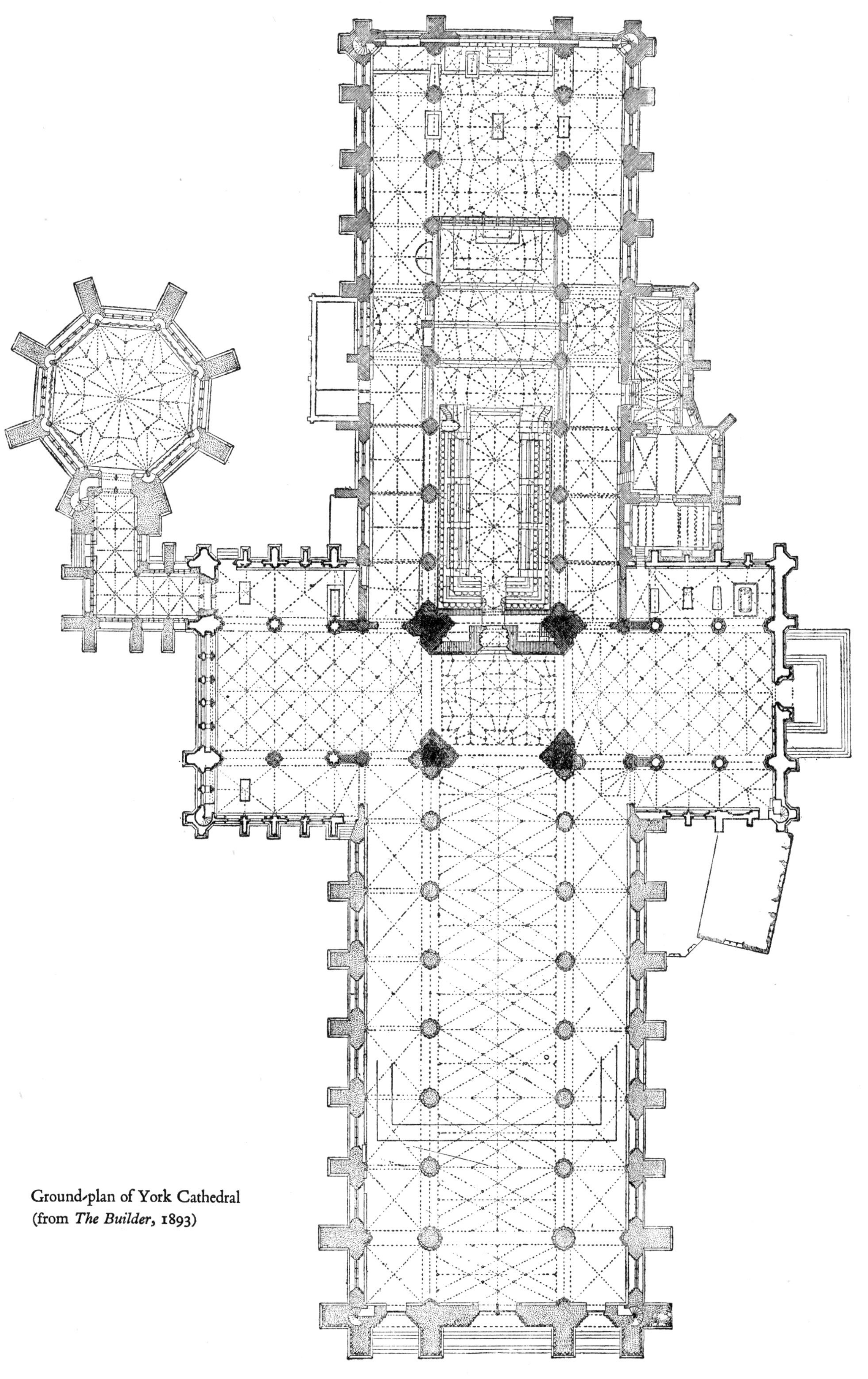

Ground-plan of York Cathedral
(from *The Builder*, 1893)

157

Figures of kings (not very remarkable in quality) in a gorgeously rich though rather monotonous choir-screen built at the end of the fifteenth century. Similar high screens surrounding the choir stalls were general abroad, though they were seldom as rich. Except in Spain they have usually been removed, even from the Catholic churches (some as early as the sixteenth century). There are exceptions, the screen, for example, in the cathedral at Albi.

DURHAM (Co. Durham), Cathedral of Christ and Our Lady

Plates 158–166

In 995 Bishop Aldun and his monks brought the body of St. Cuthbert of Lindisfarne to Durham, and so this hitherto unimportant place became the seat of the bishopric of Bernicia, which had been founded in 635. Impregnable upon a bluff surrounded on three sides by the River Wear, and set among fortified monastery buildings, this most powerful of the cathedral-abbeys rebuilt by the Normans became the bulwark of Northumbria against the warlike Scotch. Except for the choir, rebuilt in the Gothic period, and a few additions, here is a Romanesque building unusually complete. The grime of industrial surroundings darkens and emphasizes the accent of weight and mass. The small ancient city below on the Wear still preserves its charm.

Bishop William of St. Carileph began the fabric in 1093. It is one of the greatest importance in the history of architecture, since it may have been at Durham that the ribbed vault so vital to the development of Gothic was first employed—in 1096 in the south aisle of the choir. After William of St. Carileph died, funds were short. The original plan of vaulting the main and side-aisles of the choir was completed, but the builders had to give up the idea of vaulting the centre aisle. The translation of the body of St. Cuthbert into the new cathedral in 1104 provided a new impetus and they planned again to vault the whole cathedral, including the part built during the interval to take a flat roof.

The vestibule and the monastic buildings are partly Late Romanesque, partly Gothic, even as late as the sixteenth century. The old choir, which had three apses and no ambulatory, fell into decay and was replaced between 1235 and 1289 by the unusual eastern transept known as the Chapel of the Nine Altars. The choir vault and parts of the tribune have been restored.

158

The cathedral towering above the city of Durham and its old brick houses. On the left of the cathedral, the palace of the Prince-Bishops of Durham (now the University). The Wear flows along under the dark trees and below the medieval bridge. The dominating central tower is Gothic and was begun in 1416. It has lost its spire.

159

The west façade above the steep banks of the Wear. It is Romanesque, the towers and the great window having been added between the middle and end of the thirteenth century. Below the façade, the vestibule, or "Galilee", built *c.* 1175, and used as a Lady-chapel. On the right the "New Dormitory" of the monastic buildings.

160

The eastern transept, or Chapel of the Nine Altars, from the north-east. This was built between 1235 and 1289 on the site of the Romanesque choir. The tracery of the rose-window has been renewed.

161

The Gothic cloister (north-west corner), begun in 1388, and built over the west wing of the dormitorium (see Plate 159). The west towers are in part Early Gothic of the mid-thirteenth century. Notice the soberly magnificent wall of the Romanesque church. Above the windows of the aisle stretch the smaller windows of the tribune.

162

The central aisle of the nave, looking to the west. Great cylindrical pillars alternate with composite piers, all with simply formed cushion capitals. The arcade wall is over two yards thick. In place of the usual painting, patterns were cut into the pillars. The far window is Gothic of the fourteenth century.

163

The east side of the northern wing of the transept.

164

The north aisle of the nave, looking east. The ancient ribbed vault still keeps to the round arch, so that the diagonal ribs had to be stilted and the cross ribs depressed in order to achieve the more or less even roof level which was demanded here by considerations of the tribune. In the nave (Plate 162) this difficulty is overcome by making the arches of the cross ribs pointed.

165

The choir, showing the high altar and the reredos, or "Neville Screen" given by Lord Neville in 1380. This had 107 gilded and painted figures in alabaster. On the right a Romanesque pillar. The rich High Gothic (or Decorated) east bay is contemporary with the eastern transept, or Chapel of the Nine Altars, built between 1234 and 1289, which with its rose-window is visible behind the reredos.

166

The vestibule, or "Galilee", built about 1175. This unusual building is rather like the hall of a mosque, with three rows of four arches carried on twelve slim pillars.

The Norman zigzag ornament probably has an Islamic origin. The windows (cf. Plate 159) are Gothic.

CANTERBURY

CANTERBURY

CANTERBURY

CANTERBURY

CANTERBURY

CANTERBURY

CANTERBURY

CANTERBURY

CANTERBURY

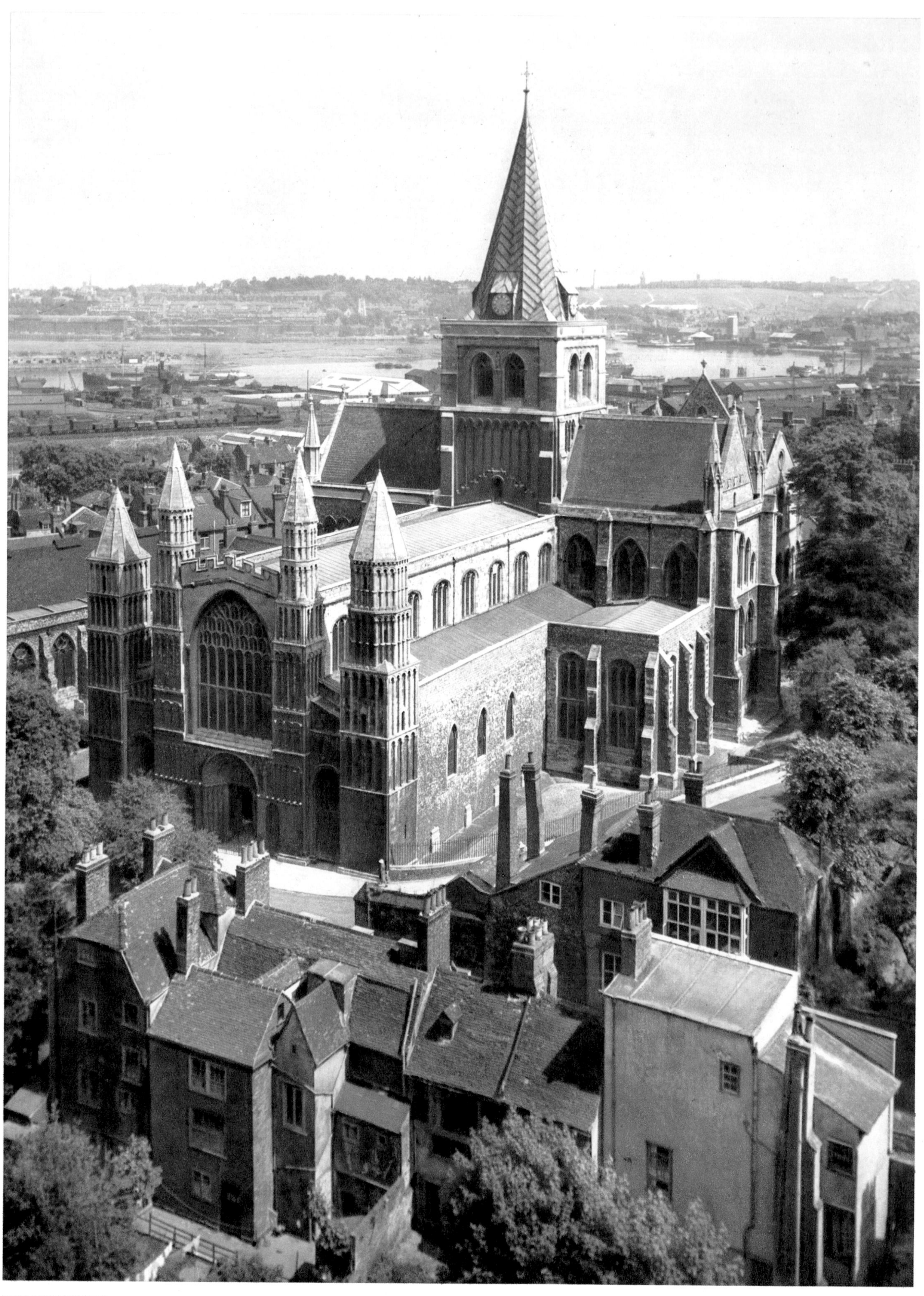

ROCHESTER

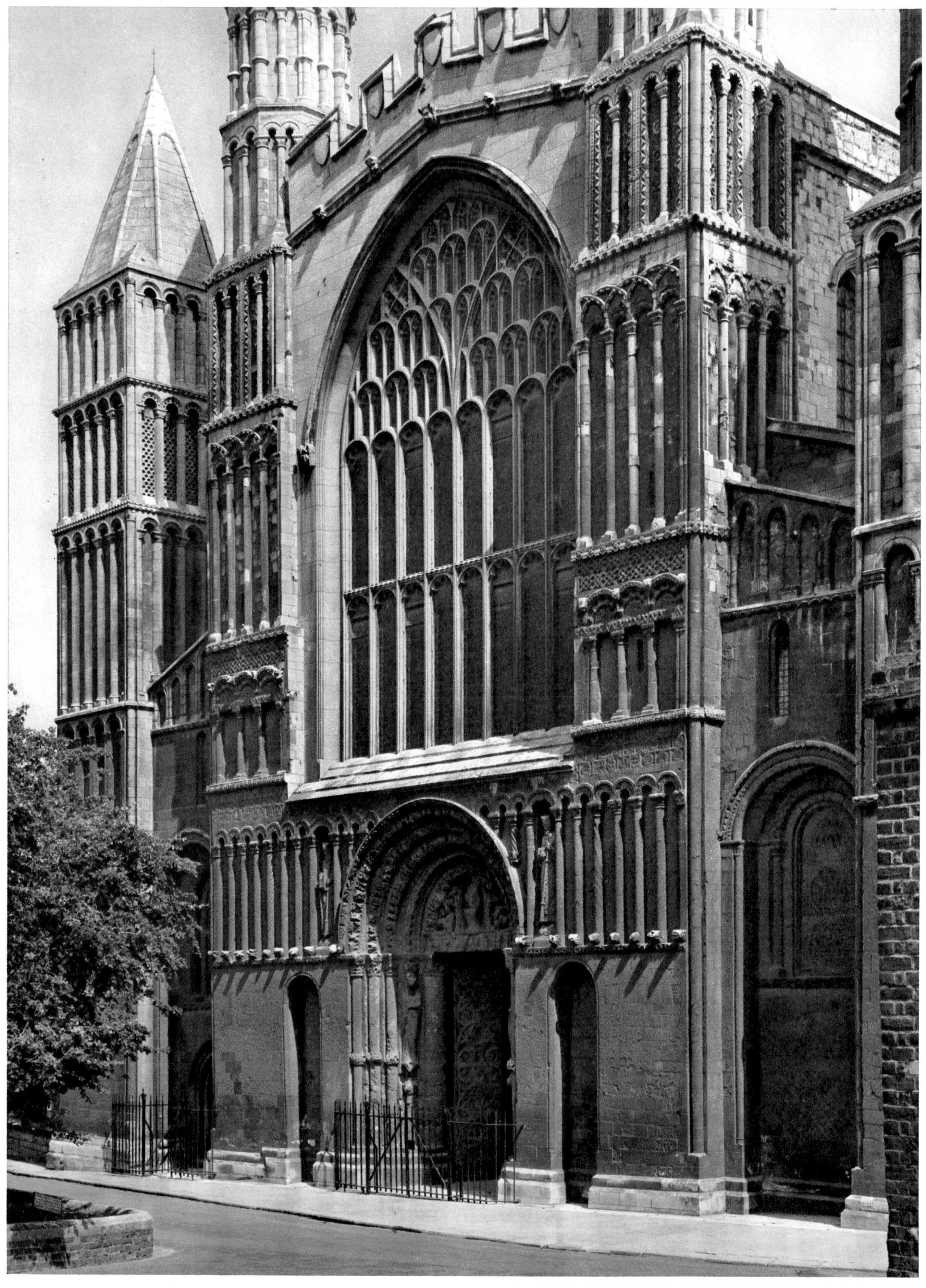

ROCHESTER

ROCHESTER

ROCHESTER 26 / 27

ST ALBANS

ST ALBANS

ST ALBANS

ST ALBANS

ELY

ELY

DOMUS·MEA·DOMUS·ORATIONIS

ELY

ELY

ELY

ELY

ELY

43

ELY

44

PETERBOROUGH

PETERBOROUGH

PETERBOROUGH

PETERBOROUGH

PETERBOROUGH

PETERBOROUGH

PETERBOROUGH

NORWICH

NORWICH

NORWICH

NORWICH

NORWICH

NORWICH

NORWICH

NORWICH

NORWICH

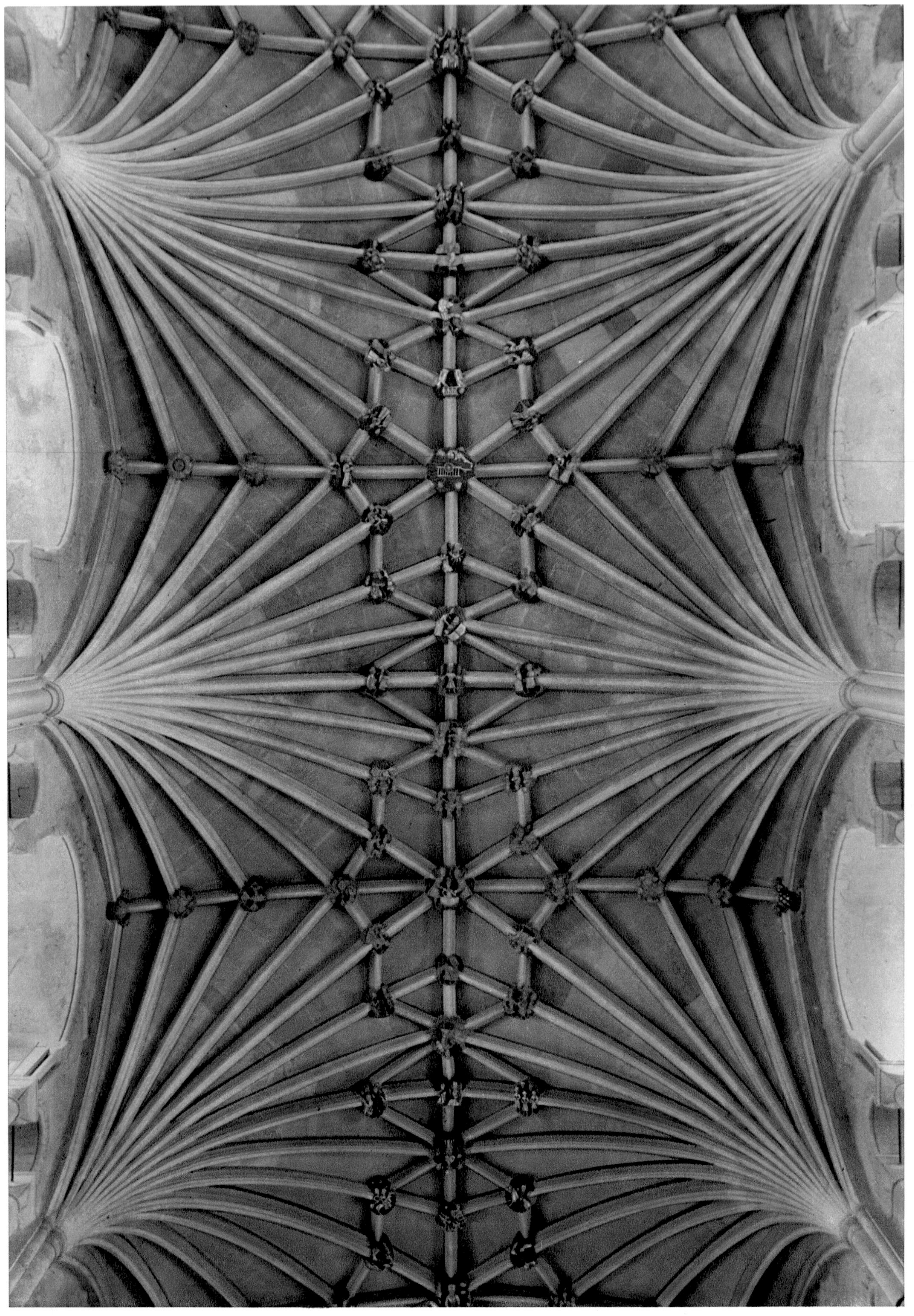

NORWICH

WINCHESTER

WINCHESTER

66

SALISBURY

67

SALISBURY

SALISBURY

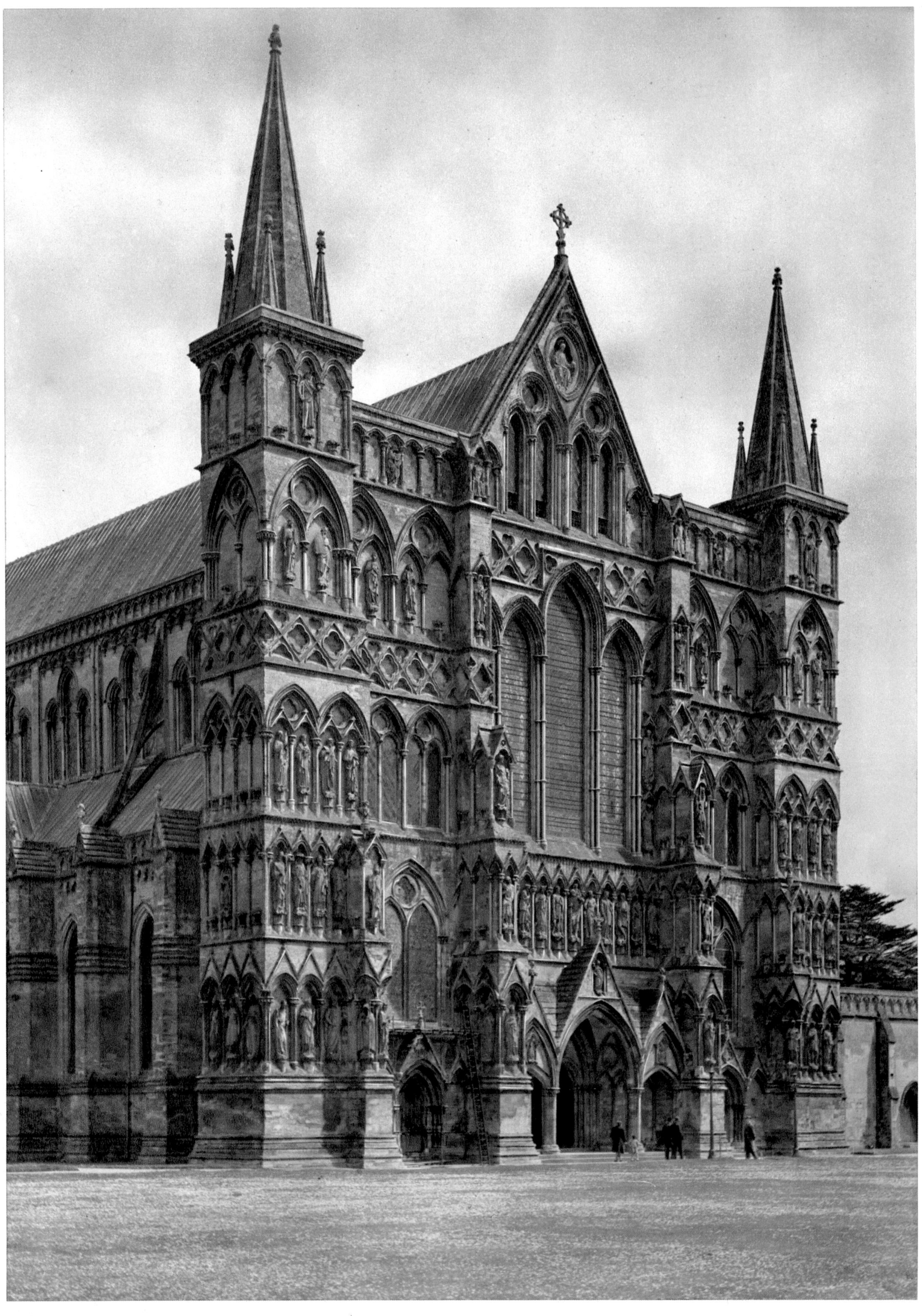

SALISBURY

SALISBURY

SALISBURY

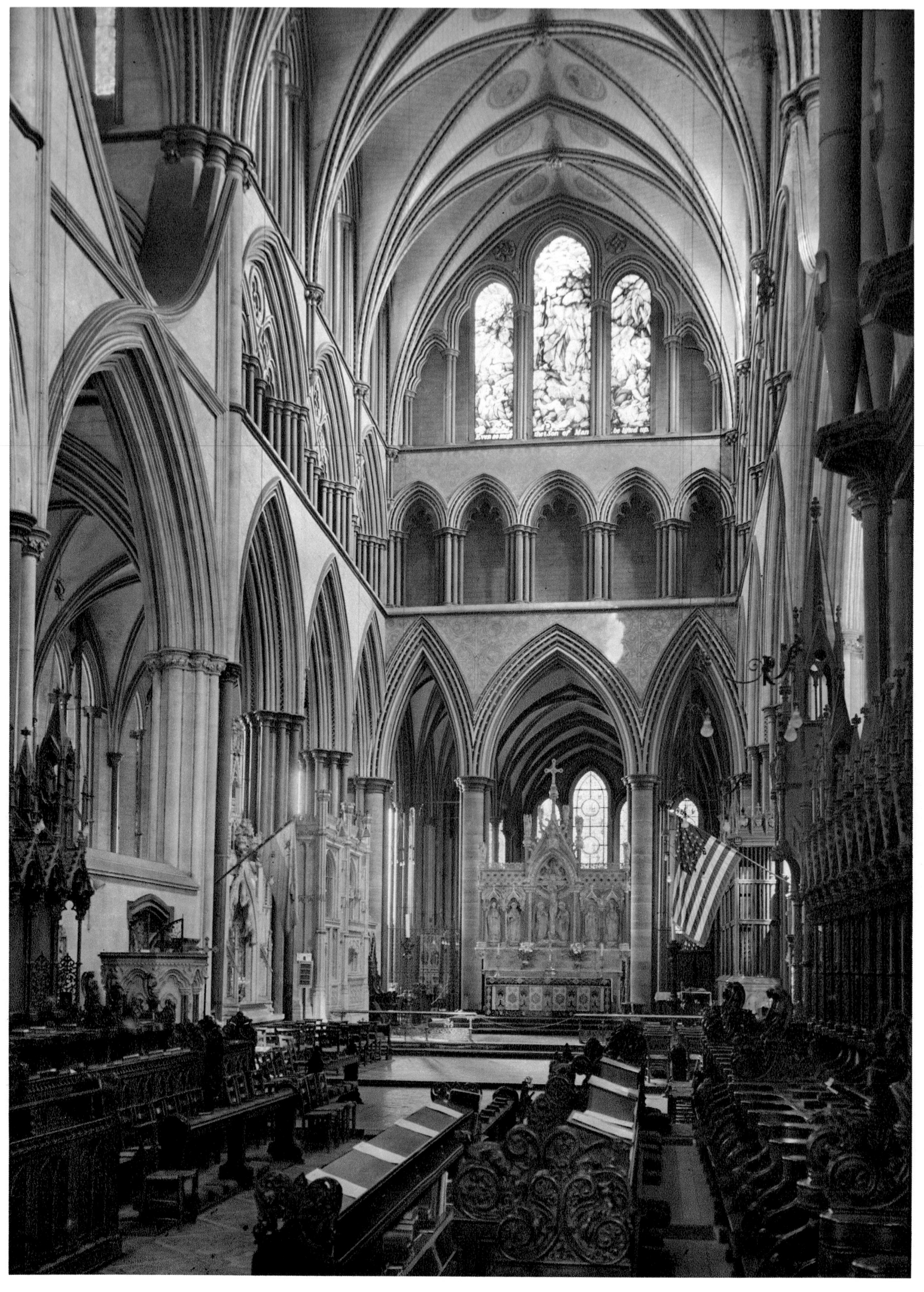
the Son of Man
be lifted up.

EXETER

EXETER

EXETER

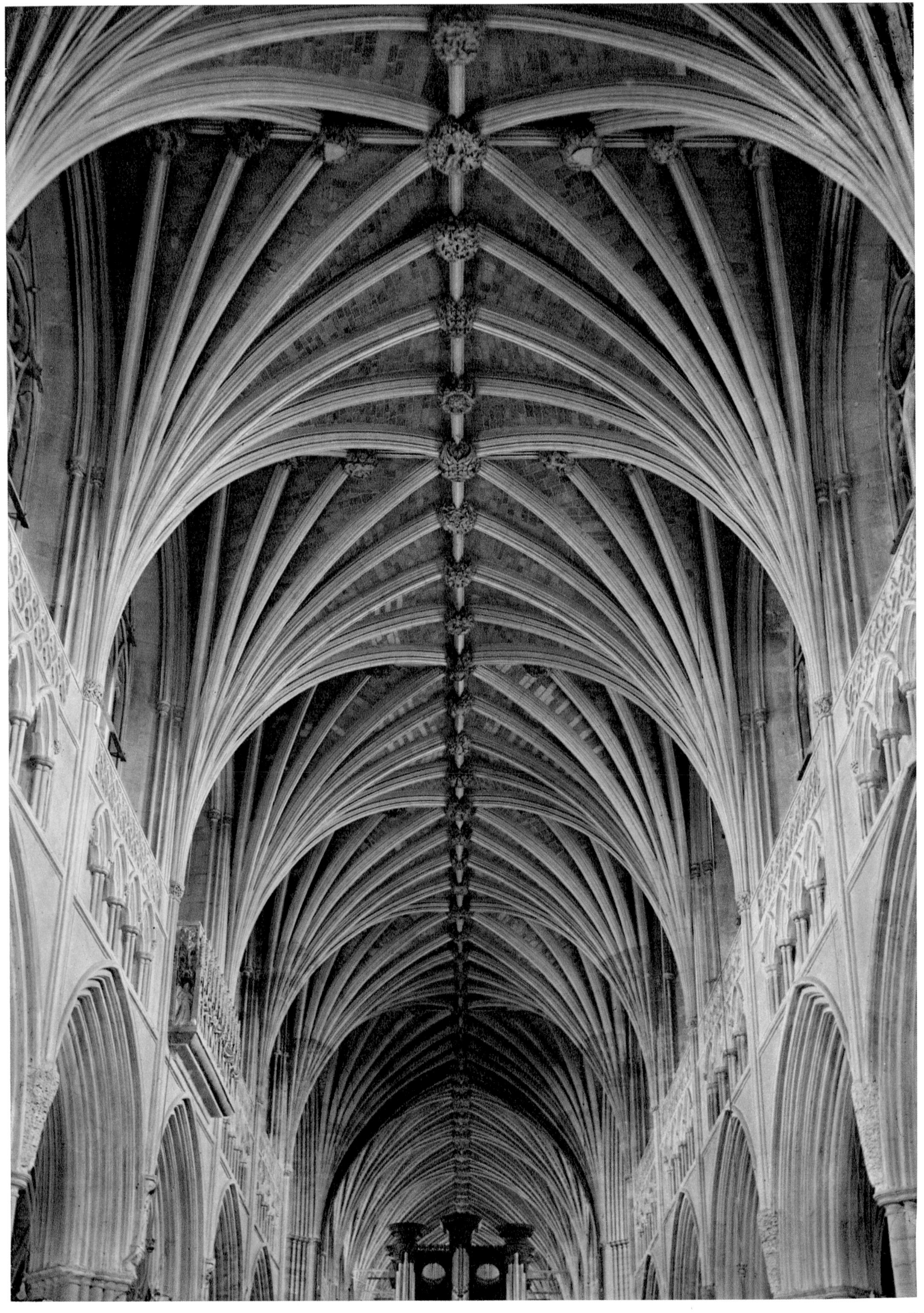

EXETER

WELLS

WELLS

81

WELLS

82

83

WELLS

84

WELLS

WELLS

WELLS

92

WELLS

93

WELLS

WELLS

WELLS

WELLS

WELLS

WELLS

WELLS

GLOUCESTER

GLOUCESTER

GLOUCESTER

GLOUCESTER

GLOUCESTER

GLOUCESTER

GLOUCESTER

GLOUCESTER

GLOUCESTER

HEREFORD

HEREFORD

HEREFORD

HEREFORD

WORCESTER

WORCESTER

WORCESTER

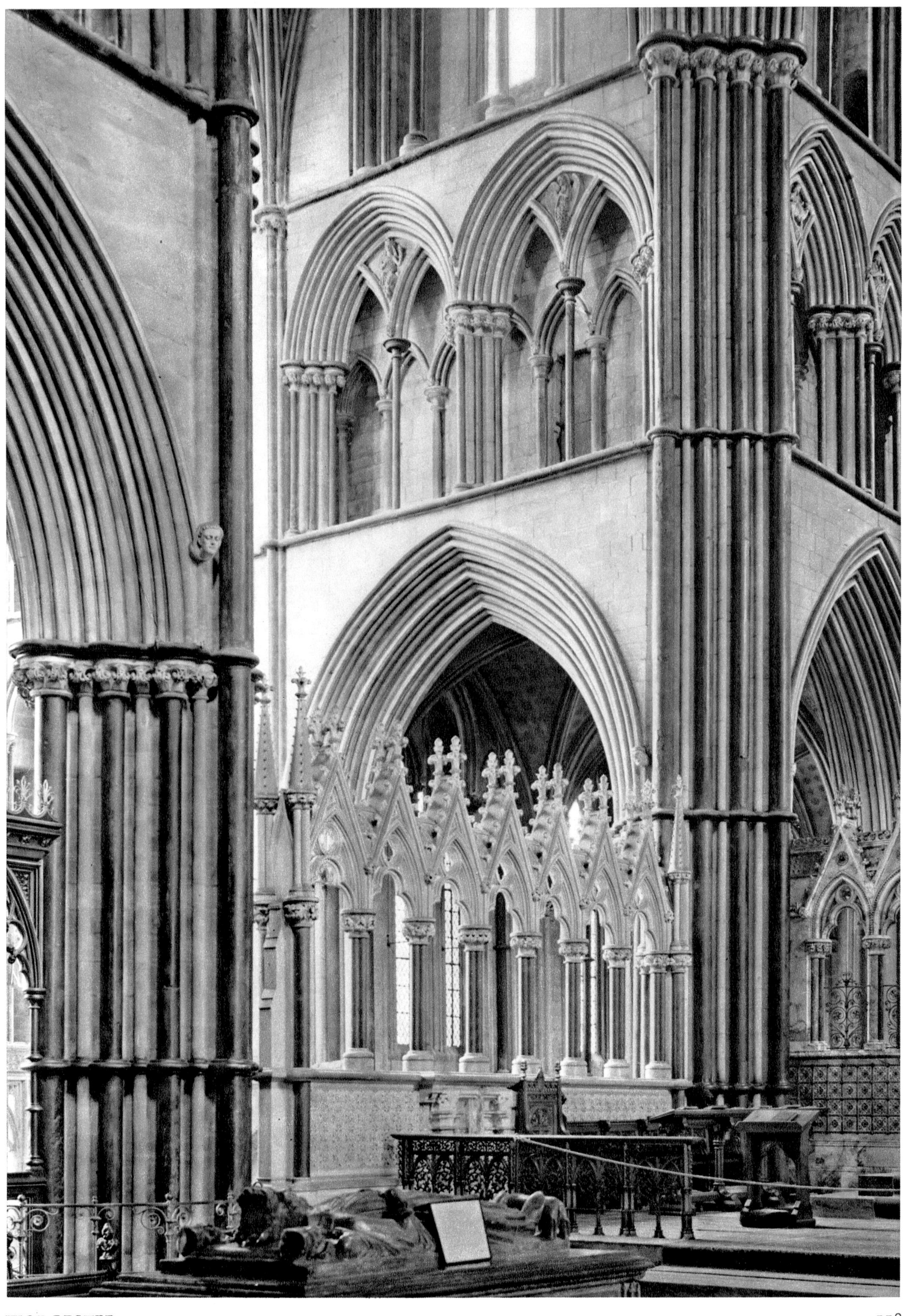

WORCESTER

WORCESTER

WORCESTER

120/123

LICHFIELD

LICHFIELD

LICHFIELD

LICHFIELD

LICHFIELD

LINCOLN

LINCOLN

132

LINCOLN

133

LINCOLN

LINCOLN

LINCOLN

LINCOLN

LINCOLN

LINCOLN

LINCOLN

LINCOLN

LINCOLN

LINCOLN

LINCOLN

146

LINCOLN

147

LINCOLN

YORK

YORK

YORK

152

YORK

153

154

YORK

155

YORK

Primus : reg an 35
Step : reg : an
Henr : Sedus : reg 35
Richus prim
Johes : reg

DURHAM

DURHAM

DURHAM

DURHAM

DURHAM

DURHAM

DURHAM

DURHAM

DURHAM